# INVITATION TO JOHN

This volume continues a new series of commentaries specially designed to answer the need for a lively, contemporary guide to the written Word. Here is the best of contemporary biblical scholarship, together with the world-renowned Jerusalem Bible text. In addition, there are study questions that will provoke and inspire further discussion.

John, the "spiritual" Gospel, is the different one, called by some the most difficult. The last of the four to be written, it was done for Christians who knew that there was now a formal break between the Jews and those who believed that Jesus was the Messiah, Christians who considered themselves a distinct group of people who had now, literally, to stand on their own. For these people, John was a reinterpreter of the traditions about Jesus, a new voice for a new era. In this Gospel we read of a special attitude toward Christ's miracles. Only when these works of Christ are seen as signs of God's presence revealed in Jesus can they lead to faith, a faith that, as John reminds us, is not a decision made once and for all but one that is active and constantly growing.

The Jesus of the Gospel of John, portrayed as one coming from the Father and returning to him, seems to be especially relevant to today's Christians as they try to understand the deeper, inner meaning of what it means to be a follower of Christ. John speaks of a renewing, ever-growing faith in Christ that constantly challenges us to look to the Father as Jesus did and to go forward into the world from the Father.

*Invitation to John* presents the Gospel and its message in a format that can be easily used for individual study, daily meditation, and/or group discussion. It is an indispensable volume for any Christian library.

# INVITATION TO JOHN

INVITATION TO SOCIOLOGY

# INVITATION TO JOHN

*A Commentary on the Gospel of John with
Complete Text from The Jerusalem Bible*

GEORGE W. MACRAE

IMAGE BOOKS
A Division of Doubleday & Company, Inc.
Garden City, New York
1978

The text of the Gospel According to John is from The Jerusalem Bible, copyright © 1966 by Darton, Longman & Todd, Ltd., and Doubleday & Company, Inc. Used by permission of the publisher.

Library of Congress Cataloging in Publication Data

MacRae, George W.
  Invitation to John.

  1. Bible. N.T. John—Commentaries. I. Bible. N.T. John. English. Jerusalem Bible. 1978.
II. Title.
BS2615.3.M26      226′.5′077
ISBN: 0-385-12212-8
Library of Congress Catalog Card Number: 77-91559

# CONTENTS

# ABBREVIATIONS OF THE BOOKS
## OF THE BIBLE

| | | | |
|---|---|---|---|
| Ac | Acts | Lk | Luke |
| Am | Amos | Lm | Lamentations |
| Ba | Baruch | Lv | Leviticus |
| 1 Ch | 1 Chronicles | 1 M | 1 Maccabees |
| 2 Ch | 2 Chronicles | 2 M | 2 Maccabees |
| 1 Co | 1 Corinthians | Mi | Micah |
| 2 Co | 2 Corinthians | Mk | Mark |
| Col | Colossians | Ml | Malachi |
| Dn | Daniel | Mt | Matthew |
| Dt | Deuteronomy | Na | Nahum |
| Ep | Ephesians | Nb | Numbers |
| Est | Esther | Ne | Nehemiah |
| Ex | Exodus | Ob | Obadiah |
| Ezk | Ezekiel | 1 P | 1 Peter |
| Ezr | Ezra | 2 P | 2 Peter |
| Ga | Galatians | Ph | Philippians |
| Gn | Genesis | Phm | Philemon |
| Hab | Habakkuk | Pr | Proverbs |
| Heb | Hebrews | Ps | Psalms |
| Hg | Haggai | Qo | Ecclesiastes |
| Ho | Hosea | Rm | Romans |
| Is | Isaiah | Rt | Ruth |
| Jb | Job | Rv | Revelation |
| Jdt | Judith | 1 S | 1 Samuel |
| Jg | Judges | 2 S | 2 Samuel |
| Jl | Joel | Sg | Song of Songs |
| Jm | James | Si | Ecclesiasticus |
| Jn | John | Tb | Tobit |
| 1 Jn | 1 John | 1 Th | 1 Thessalonians |
| 2 Jn | 2 John | 2 Th | 2 Thessalonians |
| 3 Jn | 3 John | 1 Tm | 1 Timothy |
| Jon | Jonah | 2 Tm | 2 Timothy |
| Jos | Joshua | Tt | Titus |
| Jr | Jeremiah | Ws | Wisdom |
| Jude | Jude | Zc | Zechariah |
| 1 K | 1 Kings | Zp | Zephaniah |
| 2 K | 2 Kings | | |

# GENERAL INTRODUCTION TO
# THE DOUBLEDAY NEW TESTAMENT
# COMMENTARY SERIES

Let me introduce this new commentary series on the
New Testament by sharing some experiences. In my job
as New Testament Book Review Editor for the *Catholic Biblical Quarterly,* scores of books pass through my
hands each year. As I evaluate these books and send
them out to reviewers, I cannot help but think that so
little of this scholarly research will make its way into
the hands of the educated lay person.

In talking at biblical institutes and to charismatic
and lay study groups, I find an almost unquenchable
thirst for the Word of God. People want to learn more;
they want to study. But when they ask me to rec-
ommend commentaries on the New Testament, I'm
stumped. What commentaries can I put into their
hands, commentaries that do not have the technical jar-
gon of scholars and that really communicate to the educated laity?

The goal of this popular commentary series is to
make the best of contemporary scholarship available to

the educated lay person in a highly readable and understandable way. The commentaries avoid footnotes and
other scholarly apparatus. They are short and sweet.
The authors make their points in a clear way and don't
fatigue their readers with unnecessary detail.

Another outstanding feature of this commentary
series is that it is based on The Jerusalem Bible translation, which is serialized with the commentary. This
lively and easily understandable translation has received rave reviews from millions of readers. It is the
interstate of translations and avoids the stoplights of
local-road translations.

A signal feature of the commentaries on the Gospels
is that they explore the way each evangelist used the
sayings and deeds of Jesus to meet the needs of his
church. The commentators answer the question: How
did each evangelist guide, challenge, teach, and console
the members of his community with the message of
Jesus? The commentators are not interested in the
evangelist's message for its own sake, but explain that
message with one eye on present application.

This last-mentioned feature goes hand and glove
with the innovative feature of appending Study Questions to the explanations of individual passages. By
means of these Study Questions the commentator
moves from an explanation of the message of the evangelist to a consideration of how this message might
apply to believers today.

Each commentator has two highly important qualifications: scholarly expertise and the proven ability
to communicate the results of solid scholarship to the
people of God.

I am confident that this new commentary series will

meet a real need as it helps people to unlock a door to the storehouse of God's Word where they will find food for life.

ROBERT J. KARRIS, O.F.M.
Associate Professor of New Testament Studies,
Catholic Theological Union and
Chicago Cluster of Theological Schools

# INTRODUCTION

The Fourth Gospel is different. After reading Matthew, Mark, or Luke, one finds in John a strange voice. It begins from a heavenly vantage point and speaks of a divine Word becoming flesh. It depicts a public life of Jesus that lasts several years. In it Jesus does not speak in parables and short sayings but in long, repetitive discourses. His message is not about the kingdom of God breaking into the world, but about himself coming from the Father and returning to him. Is this the same Jesus and the same good news about him?

## REINTERPRETING THE TRADITION

To understand the Fourth Gospel we must not try to harmonize it with the others. We must let its own voice speak with all its strangeness. But to do that we will have to compare it constantly with the others. Its author works with a tradition about Jesus that is also found in the other Gospels. In exactly what form he knows this tradition we are not sure. For many years interpreters have debated whether the fourth evangelist made use of Mark or Luke or all three Synoptic Gos-

pels, or whether he used the same traditions about
Jesus, in oral or written form, which the other evangelists used. The question is still not settled, but everyone
agrees that John's Gospel is basically a reinterpretation
of the tradition about Jesus. Since the Synoptic Gospels
are virtually our only other witness to this tradition, we
must refer to them constantly as we read and study
John. For the most part, the closest points of contact
will be with Mark and Luke.

## THE FACTS ABOUT THE GOSPEL

Some of the most obvious questions to ask about the
Fourth Gospel are really unanswerable. Who wrote it?
When was it written? Where was it written? For whom
was it written? The most direct answer in all cases is
that we don't know. And though it is not of primary
importance to know such facts about the Gospel, it
may be useful to indicate briefly what are the issues.

All four of the Gospels are anonymous, that is, they
themselves do not tell us who their authors were. The
Fourth Gospel indicates, as we shall see, that "the disciple Jesus loved," who figures prominently in the second half, was responsible for this Gospel, but even he is
anonymous. In the second century the names of
Matthew, Mark, Luke, and John were attached to the
Gospels, and near the end of the century John was
identified as the Apostle John. It is unlikely that the
Fourth Gospel as we have it was written by an apostle,
but it may embody a tradition of interpreting Jesus that
originated with an apostle, and of course we can neither prove nor disprove that it was John. For the sake
of convenience we will continue to call the evangelist

"John" without making any particular claims about the author.

The Fourth Gospel has been traditionally regarded as the latest of the four, and there is widespread agreement that it was written near the end of the first century A.D. As we shall see in discussing chapter 9 in particular, it presupposes a situation in which there had been a formal breach between the Jewish synagogue and those who believed Jesus was the Messiah. Such a situation most likely developed in the 80s or 90s. The Gospel can't be much later, however, because there is a manuscript fragment of it datable to the early second century. The question of date, like that of author, is bound up with the history of the composition of the Gospel, to which we must turn in a moment.

As for where the Gospel was written, any suggestion would be little more than a guess. Greek was in use throughout the Mediterranean world, and thus the language gives no clue. The question of whom it was written for is more appropriate. Some have thought the Gospel of John was written as a kind of missionary document to convert Jews or pagans to Christianity. Its polemical tone makes this unlikely, however, and much recent scholarly study has focused on the Johannine church as a distinct group of Christians for whom this was "their" Gospel. They are a church that has its roots in Judaism but that has recently been rejected by the Jews. They seem also to be conscious of their own identity vis-à-vis other Christian churches.

## THE PROCESS OF COMPOSITION

The student of the Fourth Gospel has to be aware of a complex set of questions about how the Gospel came into being in the form in which we find it in our Bible. There are signs that it has been tampered with, so to speak, in its history, and some awareness of the problems will help us understand it better.

First, there are signs that we may call textual problems, additions to the text of the Gospel made by ancient copyists who aided in spreading the work throughout the church in the early centuries. For example, the moving story of the woman taken in adultery, which has for centuries appeared as John 7:53 to 8:11, is not found in the oldest and best manuscripts of the Gospel and is certainly not an original part of it. The same can be said of John 5:3b–4, which introduces an angel of the Lord into the story of the paralytic at the pool (see the commentary on this passage).

Secondly, there are indications of additions made to the Gospel before it was circulated, passages which seem secondary but are not absent from any ancient manuscripts. The most widely recognized example is chapter 21, which is added to the Gospel after the formal conclusion at 20:30–31. In content and to some extent in style, this appendix or epilogue is not part of the evangelist's original work, and indeed it does not actually claim to be (see 21:24). Other editorial additions to the text are not so obvious, but recognizing them is important for following the original plan of the book. Two further examples are 12:44–50 and 6:55b–59 (see the commentary on these passages). The presence of such additions to the text indicates that at least one second hand was at work in producing the final form of the Gospel, which is therefore the result of a process of composition. Many think the process consisted of multiple stages from the first formation

of Johannine insights into Jesus to the final addition of
the appendix.

Thirdly, there are very probably dislocations of passages within the Gospel. One of the greatest of modern
commentators on John, the late Rudolf Bultmann (*The
Gospel of John,* German original 1941, English translation 1971), believed that passages throughout the Gospel had been accidentally misplaced, and as a result he
completely reorganized the Gospel in his commentary.
Most scholars have not followed Bultmann in this respect, since there is a danger of improving upon the
evangelist's logic and failing to recognize what the Gospel actually says. Yet, though we can't explain how it
happened, there may be some dislocation of passages.
In this commentary we will argue for only one instance.
Chapters 5 and 6 seem on several grounds to be in the
wrong order (see the commentary on 5:1–18).

## SOURCES OF THE GOSPEL

John was a reinterpreter of the traditions about Jesus
and he certainly was familiar with much that went into
the Synoptic Gospels. He may even have known one or
more of these Gospels themselves. But quite apart from
this issue, there continues to be a great deal of discussion about other sources used by the evangelist, especially for those parts of his Gospel which do not have
an obvious counterpart in the Synoptics. The most obvious of these consists of the long discourses of Jesus,
which are characterized by a kind of dualistic language
—light and darkness, above and below, truth and false-
hood—and a pattern of talking about Christ ("Christology") as the one who descends from the Father into

the world and reascends to the Father. This sounds like gnostic language—that of a radically antiworldly religious movement, prominent in the second century, which had its Christian version but was generally regarded as heretical. It was again Bultmann who suggested that John took over a collection of pagan gnostic discourses and adapted them to Jesus. Again, few have accepted this suggestion, but its merit has been to call our attention to the peculiar character of the discourses. It is more likely that John was simply influenced by the style and language of revelation literature current in the Greco-Roman world. John did not intend his work to be gnostic; his emphasis on the real humanity of Jesus rules that out. But his reinterpretation was tending toward a position which the Christian gnostics found congenial.

There are clues in the Gospel that suggest another source may have been used. John 2:11 speaks of "the first of the signs given by Jesus," and 4:54 mentions "the second sign given by Jesus." These passages have led many interpreters, again including Bultmann, to the view that the evangelist had a "signs source," a collection of miracle stories about Jesus, which he incorporated into his Gospel. Some of the stories would have had their synoptic counterpart, like the multiplication of the loaves in 6:1–15, and others would have been quite original, like the wine miracle at Cana in 2:1–11. This source, though of course only hypothetical, is much more likely to have been used. What will be most important for us, however, is to see how it is used. The Fourth Gospel has a very special attitude toward miracles, which it calls "signs." When they are perceived only as miracles, they do not lead to faith in Jesus. Only when they are seen as signs of God's presence revealed in Jesus can they lead to faith. In the first half of the Gospel especially, the reactions of people to the signs are sharply contrasted with their reactions to the revealing *word* of Jesus.

## BACKGROUND OF THE GOSPEL

We have already mentioned the view of some interpreters that the Fourth Gospel has its background in gnosticism. That view is itself to be rejected, but one can acknowledge that the Gospel is influenced by the kind of religious language that later was recognized as characteristically gnostic. It is much more important to acknowledge that the background of the Gospel is first and foremost the Old Testament. Like most early Christians, the author, or various authors, was thoroughly steeped in Old Testament language and imagery and in a tradition of interpreting it. The modern reader of John, as of the whole New Testament, needs to recognize Old Testament themes, quotations, and allusions to appreciate what is being said. In the commentary we will call attention to a number of these, and the reader should not hesitate to look up the passages.

The situation of the Johannine church, expelled from the synagogue, suggests that the author's background was primarily Jewish, but it is difficult to be more specific about what kind of Judaism. In view of some important similarities with the language of the Dead Sea Scrolls, some have thought of a Judaism directly influenced by the Essenes of Palestine. But this is on other grounds unlikely. The similarities of language show only that the Essenes too were influenced by the Greco-Roman milieu. Wherever John's Jewish roots

are to be found, he is quite consciously aware of the
Greco-Roman world he lives in. He writes in Greek
(though with traces of a Hebrew or Aramaic background for some traditions) and uses a number of techniques from contemporary classical literature. His
choice of symbols and images seems often to be based
on their universal appeal to Christians of either Jewish
or gentile background. The world that cradled the early
church was a complex one in which many religious cur-
rents interacted. The Fourth Gospel is above all a
product of that world.

## WHY READ THE FOURTH GOSPEL?

If the Fourth Gospel is so markedly different from
the other Gospels, what is its value to the modern
Christian? Of course the answer to such a question can
only be formulated when one has read and studied the
Gospel itself. And it should be formulated in a personal
manner by each reader. At the least, one will read John
because it is there; it is part of the New Testament and
therefore of the Christian heritage. But throughout its
history, from the time it was labeled "the spiritual Gospel" in the early third century, it has exercised an
enormous appeal to its readers. Each one will have to
judge whether that appeal makes worthwhile the effort
needed to understand it first of all in its own terms.

Here is one suggestion. The Gospel of John reflects
an understanding of God and the world in which everything is drawn in sharp lines. There are radical choices
to be made within the framework of opposites in cosmic conflict. But the challenge is always personal, even

individual. John serves to remind the Christian that underlying all the legitimate and necessary preoccupations of Christian life, there is the personal, existential attitude of faith, not as a decision to be made once and for all, but as an act that is always present when the believer realizes that God is encountered in the humanity of Jesus.

## STUDY SUGGESTIONS

The Fourth Gospel is also distinctive in that it presupposes from the outset that the reader knows the whole story. In a very general way most Christian readers do know it, but John makes many specific allusions to what is to come later. It would be very useful therefore to read the whole Gospel text through quickly at the outset, then to begin studying it passage by passage. And in the study, it would be very helpful to have access to a copy of the whole Bible. There are many references in the following pages, particularly to the Old Testament and to the Synoptic Gospels. For a rewarding study of John one should look them up and compare.

The Jerusalem Bible translation (abbreviated JB) is an eloquent one in many passages. But like any translation of the Bible, it incorporates the interpretations of its editors and translators. There will be times when we disagree with the text which the JB reads or with the translation. These instances should not be merely a distraction but an opportunity to come to grips with the biblical text and evaluate some options for understanding it.

## ACKNOWLEDGMENTS

The commentator has learned from three sources mainly, and they must be acknowledged if only with a word. First, he has learned from countless great scholars whose work has shed light on the meaning of John. The great commentaries of Bultmann and Raymond E. Brown have been particularly helpful. Secondly, he has learned from his students, whose interest and enthusiasm for the Gospel have produced valuable insights. Thirdly, he has learned from reading and rereading the text of the Gospel itself. It never seems to fail to unlock more of its own secrets. For the friendly advice of the editor, Robert J. Karris, the author expresses his appreciation. And to Dorothy Riehm, who prepared the manuscript with meticulous care, he expresses his thanks.

GEORGE W. MACRAE, S.J.
Harvard Divinity School
January 17, 1978

EDITOR'S NOTE: Sometimes there is a discrepancy between the numbering of chapters and verses in The Jerusalem Bible and that in some other versions. In such cases The Jerusalem Bible citation is given first, followed by the alternative citation—e.g., Ml 3:23 (= 4:5).

INVITATION TO JOHN

*The Prologue*
John 1:1–18

## John 1:1-18
## OVERTURE

1 In the beginning was the Word:
   the Word was with God
   and the Word was God.
2   He was with God in the beginning.
3   Through him all things came to be,
    not one thing had its being but through him.
4   All that came to be had life in him
    and that life was the light of men,
5   a light that shines in the dark,
    a light that darkness could not overpower.

6   A man came, sent by God.
    His name was John.
7   He came as a witness,
    as a witness to speak for the light,
    so that everyone might believe through him.
8   He was not the light,
    only a witness to speak for the light.

9   The Word was the true light
    that enlightens all men;
    and he was coming into the world.
10  He was in the world
    that had its being through him,
    and the world did not know him.
11  He came to his own domain
    and his own people did not accept him.

12    But to all who did accept him
      he gave power to become children of God,
      to all who believe in the name of him

13    who was born not out of human stock
      or urge of the flesh
      or will of man
      but of God himself.

14    The Word was made flesh,
      he lived among us,
      and we saw his glory,
      the glory that is his as the only Son of the
          Father,
      full of grace and truth.

15    John appears as his witness. He proclaims:
      "This is the one of whom I said:
      He who comes after me
      ranks before me
      because he existed before me."

16    Indeed, from his fullness we have, all of us, re-
          ceived—
      yes, grace in return for grace,

17    since, though the Law was given through Moses,
      grace and truth have come through Jesus
          Christ.

18    No one has ever seen God;
      it is the only Son, who is nearest to the Father's
          heart,
      who has made him known.

☩

Interpreters of John are in wide (though not unanimous) agreement that the Gospel begins by fusing a
poem or hymn with the story. They disagree equally
widely about which verses belong to the hymn, but

what is important is the cosmic perspective ("In the beginning," cf. Gn 1:1) with which the author introduces the pre-existent divine Son, the Word. Verses 6-8 and 15 are certainly interpolations in the hymn; in fact, if one began the story with them, the Gospel would begin very much like Mark, and the hymn itself would appear to be the interpolation. The evangelist is clearly joining a timeless theological perspective to the story of Jesus.

The hymn, which may have its origin in a non-Christian poem about a heavenly revealer of God, moves from an assertion of the divine origin of the Word to a witness of the Christian community's faith in him as embodied in Jesus. The movement is from the majestic "in the beginning was the Word" to the personal "we saw his glory." For a similar hymnic development, see the famous christological hymn in Philippians 2:6-11. No poetic scheme can account for all the verses here in John, since some of them, besides the interpolations mentioned, appear to be explanatory (e.g., 1:13, and perhaps 1:17-18). What holds the poetic structure together, though not with rigorous consistency, is the linking of key words such as *Word, God, be, life, light,* etc.

Whatever the exact literary designation of the Gospel prologue, Ruldolf Bultmann and others are no doubt on the mark in calling it an "overture" to the Gospel. It introduces a whole succession of themes that are developed in the chapters that follow: the Word, life, light and darkness, witness, the world, and many others. In verses 11 and 12 there is an outline of the major divisions of the Gospel itself: Chapters 1 to 12 dramatize the coming of Jesus to "his own" and his rejection by most of them, and chapters 13 to 20 detail the effect of his coming on those who do accept him, the disciples, who are privileged to become children of God (see the commentary on 20:17).

Why is Jesus called the Word, especially since he is not called that anywhere else in the Gospel? In fact, in the later history of Christology in the Christian tradition, the title "Word" has played a central role for which the Johannine prologue is the sole witness. Here is the appropriate place to make a general observation: The Fourth Gospel presumes from the beginning that the reader knows the story. To test this insight, one should study the first twelve chapters and then return to the prologue. The reader would then perceive that Jesus is indeed the Word in the sense that his mission is to reveal the Father and even to embody the word of this revelation. In fact, as the Gospel unfolds, it will become clear that there is a decided emphasis on faith in Jesus on the basis of word in contrast to miracle. The readers of the Gospel, for whom the historical activity of Jesus is in the past, have only the word of gospel proclamation, but it is a major part of the intention of John to declare that this is not a second-best: "Happy are those who have not seen and yet believe" (20:29).

Centuries of interpretation of John have recognized that the central focus of the opening passage is on verse 14, the statement of the incarnation. Part of it may be literally rendered, with an explicit allusion to the dwelling of Yahweh among his people in the desert, as "he pitched his tent among us." How we read this verse makes all the difference in the world for understanding Johannine Christology. It is possible, though perhaps less likely, to understand the statement to mean nothing more than that God visited his people. The alternative

is to confront the paradox that the eternally pre-existent divine Word actually entered into human, fleshly,
existence. The implication of the latter understanding,
that the human is revelatory of the divine, is more radical, more difficult, and very likely more faithful to the
perspective of John.

A few details of interpretation are in order. In verse
1 the text does not unambiguously identify the Word
(the Son, Christ) with God but asserts divinity without
challenging the monotheism of early Christian faith; the
New English Bible very attractively translates "and
what God was, the Word was." Secondly, the division
between verses 3 and 4 has from ancient times been
problematic. The traditional rendering, most probably
under the influence of christological controversies of
the fourth century, is "not one thing that came to be
had its being but through him." But the JB text is preferable. In verse 13, however, the JB opts with a minor-
ity of ancient versions to understand the qualifications
stated there to refer to the divine origin of Jesus. It is
textually sounder, and in better harmony with Johannine theology, to accept the majority reading of the
manuscripts: "to all who believe in his name, who were
born. . . ." Verse 13 thus refers to those mentioned in
verse 12. Finally, the phrase "the only Son" in verse 18
is problematic because the better manuscripts from antiquity say "the only God." One can understand the
reluctance of early Christians to call Jesus "God" out-
rightly, but it may be that Johannine Christology is developed to the point of doing just that (cf. 1:1 and
20:28).

The splendor of the prologue to the Gospel must
never be lost in exegetical details. It inaugurates the
message of the Gospel on a level unparalleled in the

gospel tradition. In the human, the limited experience of humans, the evangelist sees the divine presence, and perhaps this is his major insight into the story of Jesus. The unfolding of the story will tell.

STUDY QUESTIONS: How can the human be a revelation of the divine? Do we experience such a revelation in our own lives? Would it make a difference if Jesus were only a man or "only God"?

*The Book of Signs*
John 1:19 to 12:50

## Introduction to John 1:19 to 12:50
## THE BOOK OF SIGNS

Discovering the principles that determine the structure of the Fourth Gospel has long fascinated its interpreters. The problem is not that there are few of them or that they are hard to find, but rather that there are so many and that they interlock in complex patterns. The feast days of the Jewish calendar, Jesus' journeys between Galilee and Jerusalem, his miracles and his discourses, the contexts of his revealing word—these and other principles of structure have been detected.

But there is one arrangement of the Gospel we can not ignore, and that is the sharp division between chapters 12 and 13. This structures the work in two main parts dealing with Jesus' public ministry, in which he reveals himself to the world at large, and the passion-resurrection story, in which he reveals himself in a new way to his followers. A similar structure, though not rigorously carried out, is found in Mark, where the new section begins at Mark 8:22.

The Book of Signs, as C. H. Dodd has called chapters 1 to 12, is dominated not only by the miracles of Jesus, culminating in the raising of Lazarus from the dead, but also by the discourses of Jesus. Most of these produce conflict with those whom the evangelist calls "the Jews," and the tension mounts in reaction to both discourse and sign until Jesus' death becomes certain.

Running through the Book of Signs are a number of theological issues of great importance for this Gospel. One has to do with the miracles of Jesus, the "signs," which are portrayed as an inadequate basis for faith unless they are properly perceived. True faith in Jesus is a response to his revealing word. Another issue centers around the use of titles to understand the identity of Jesus. In several scenes we will note a progression from recognizing Jesus as the (or a) prophet or as the Messiah to seeing him as the Son of Man or in some other light. Jesus' true identity was of course made known in the prologue, but it is presented as an issue for the characters in the Gospel and it must have been the subject of discussion in the Johannine church as well. The reader of the Book of Signs should be alert to clues about signs, words, and faith and to the role of christological titles.

## John 1:19-34
# A VOICE THAT CRIES
# IN THE WILDERNESS

<sup>19</sup> This is how John appeared as a witness. When the Jews sent priests and Levites from Jerusalem <sup>20</sup> to ask him, "Who are you?" ·he not only declared, but he declared quite openly, "I am not the <sup>21</sup> Christ." ·"Well then," they asked, "are you Elijah?" "I am not," he said. "Are you the Prophet?" <sup>22</sup> He answered, "No." ·So they said to him, "Who are you? We must take back an answer to those who sent us. What have you to say about your-<sup>23</sup> self?" ·So John said, "I am, as Isaiah prophesied:

a voice that cries in the wilderness:
Make a straight way for the Lord."

<sup>24</sup> Now these men had been sent by the Pharisees, <sup>25</sup> and they put this further question to him, "Why are you baptizing if you are not the Christ, and <sup>26</sup> not Elijah, and not the prophet?" ·John replied, "I baptize with water; but there stands among <sup>27</sup> you—unknown to you—·the one who is coming after me; and I am not fit to undo his sandal <sup>28</sup> strap." ·This happened at Bethany, on the far side of the Jordan, where John was baptizing.

<sup>29</sup> The next day, seeing Jesus coming toward him, John said, "Look, there is the lamb of God that

30 takes away the sin of the world. ·This is the one I
spoke of when I said: A man is coming after me
who ranks before me because he existed before
31 me. ·I did not know him myself, and yet it was to
reveal him to Israel that I came baptizing with
32 water." ·John also declared, "I saw the Spirit coming down on him from heaven like a dove and
33 resting on him. ·I did not know him myself, but
he who sent me to baptize with water had said to
me, 'The man on whom you see the Spirit come
down and rest is the one who is going to baptize
34 with the Holy Spirit.' ·Yes, I have seen and I am
the witness that he is the Chosen One of God."

✠

The opening scenes in the Gospel are clearly set off
by the evangelist in four episodes, the last three introduced by the recurring phrase "the next day" (verses
29, 35, 43). The first two center on John the Baptist
and his witness to Jesus; the last two, treated below,
focus on the first disciples.

The evangelist's thorough reinterpretation of the traditions about Jesus is quite visible at the outset. To see
what he is reinterpreting, the reader might look at
Mark 1:1–11, where we find the appearance and ministry of John, his role described in terms of Isaiah 40:3,
his "prophecy" of the one to come after him, and his
baptism of Jesus. In the Fourth Gospel the baptism of
Jesus is alluded to but not actually mentioned. This ret-
icence may be part of a more general tendency in the
Gospel to play down the Baptist by not appearing to
make Jesus depend on him. Some think there were still

followers of the Baptist in touch with the Johannine community and needing to be put in their place.

John the Baptist plays a very important role, however, as witness to Jesus' identity. Note how the word "witness" is used in verses 19 and 34 (and in Greek in verse 32), framing the scenes. He denies that he is the Christ—the Greek term, before it became a name of Jesus, translated "Messiah," as John reminds us in 1:41—or Elijah (see Ml 3:23–24 [= 4:5–6]) or the prophet (see Dt 18:15). In thus reinterpreting the theme of speculating on the identity of Jesus (see Mk 6:14–15 and 8:27–28, where some think Jesus is John the Baptist come back to life), the evangelist focuses our attention on Jesus himself, and that is the Baptist's real function (see the commentary on 3:22–36). Witnessing to Jesus is important to this Gospel. Not only does the Baptist do it, but the evangelist himself does also (see for example 19:35).

The theme that binds together all four "days" to the opening of the Gospel is the concentration on the person of Jesus—what is called Johannine Christocentrism —under the rubric of a succession of christological titles. Each of the four "days" introduces its own list of titles, and the cumulative effect is to see a large part of the early church's faith in Jesus laid out before us at the outset of the story.

Besides the titles used negatively about himself in the first scene, the Baptist calls Jesus "the lamb of God that takes away the sin of the world." The specific background of this unique designation is hard to identify, but it may refer to the role of the suffering servant of God in Isaiah 52:13 to 53:12. To determine exactly what constitutes the world's sin in this Gospel we shall have to be alert to the development of the idea of sin in the following chapters. The Baptist also calls Jesus by the messianic title "the Chosen One of God"; in some of the ancient manuscripts the reading is "the Son of God." In either case, the background of the title is the baptism of Jesus in which God acknowledges his Son-Messiah.

STUDY QUESTION: What kind of witness to the identity of Jesus is the modern Christian called upon to make?

# John 1:35–51
## WHAT DO YOU WANT?

35 On the following day as John stood there again
36 with two of his disciples, ·Jesus passed, and John
stared hard at him and said, "Look, there is the
37 lamb of God." ·Hearing this, the two disciples
38 followed Jesus. ·Jesus turned around, saw them
following and said, "What do you want?" They
answered, "Rabbi,"—which means Teacher—
39 "where do you live?" ·"Come and see," he replied;
so they went and saw where he lived, and stayed
with him the rest of that day. It was about the
tenth hour.
40 One of these two who became followers of
Jesus after hearing what John had said was An-
41 drew, the brother of Simon Peter. ·Early next
morning, Andrew met his brother and said to him,
"We have found the Messiah"—which means the
42 Christ—·and he took Simon to Jesus. Jesus looked
hard at him and said, "You are Simon son of John;
you are to be called Cephas"—meaning Rock.
43 The next day, after Jesus had decided to leave
for Galilee, he met Philip and said, "Follow me."
44 Philip came from the same town, Bethsaida, as
45 Andrew and Peter. ·Philip found Nathanael and
said to him, "We have found the one Moses wrote
about in the Law, the one about whom the
prophets wrote: he is Jesus son of Joseph, from

<sup>46</sup> Nazareth." ·"From Nazareth?" said Nathanael.
"Can anything good come from that place?"
<sup>47</sup> "Come and see," replied Philip. ·When Jesus saw
Nathanael coming he said of him, "There is an
Israelite who deserves the name, incapable of
<sup>48</sup> deceit." ·"How do you know me?" said Nathan-
ael. "Before Philip came to call you," said Jesus,
<sup>49</sup> "I saw you under the fig tree." ·Nathanael an-
swered, "Rabbi, you are the Son of God, you are
<sup>50</sup> the King of Israel." ·Jesus replied, "You believe
that just because I said: I saw you under the fig
<sup>51</sup> tree. You will see greater things than that." ·And
then he added, "I tell you most solemnly, you will
see heaven laid open and, above the Son of Man,
the angels of God ascending and descending."

☦

The third and fourth "days" of the Gospel beginning
are closely symmetrical ("early next morning" in verse
41 is an interpretative translation; it is not clear that
the evangelist wanted to add another day here). In
each case the first disciple called, Andrew or Philip, is
impelled to invite another, Peter or Nathanael, to follow Jesus. A similar dynamic will occur in chapter 4,
where the woman at the well undertakes the missionary
task of calling the people of her town to believe in
Jesus. Discovery of Jesus' identity, even if not yet ade-
quate understanding of him, implies a desire to share
the news.

The traditions being reinterpreted here are the "call
stories" or accounts of a vocation to discipleship. In
Mark 1:16–20 there are two stories of the call of
Simon (Peter) and Andrew and of James and John.

Our evangelist dramatizes such traditional stories in his
own way, but his emphasis is still on following, that is,
being a disciple of, Jesus. Note the use of the word
"follow" in verses 37, 38, 40, 43. The invitation to become a disciple-believer is in the form "Come and see,"
whether on the lips of Jesus himself or of another disciple. Coupled with the opening words of Jesus in the
Gospel, the question "What do you want?," these remarks also serve as an invitation to the Gospel itself,
where the revealing word of Jesus is to be found.

The main emphasis of the two stories is still on the
person of Jesus and the titles used by early Christians
to express their faith in him. Jesus is Rabbi, Messiah,
the prophet, Son of God, and King of Israel. It is characteristic of the Christocentrism of this Gospel that
Jesus himself is called king instead of being portrayed
as preaching about the kingdom of God as in the other
Gospels. Nathanael's remarkable confession of faith in
Jesus as Messiah is in response to the apparently super-
human insight Jesus displays. The "greater things" that
he is about to see include the following incident at
Cana and indeed all the signs to come.

The evangelist has added a saying about the Son of
Man here to introduce another important christological
title. The saying is addressed to a wider audience (plural "you" in Greek) that of course includes the readers
of the Gospel. It boldly combines allusions to Jacob's
ladder (Gn 28:12) and the heavenly Son of Man (Dn
7:13) to suggest that the heavenly glory of the divine
Son will be visible on earth.

STUDY QUESTIONS: What do we seek in approaching
                 Jesus? How does the discovery of
                 his identity affect our lives?

## John 2:1–12
## THE FIRST OF THE SIGNS

<sup>1</sup> 2 Three days later there was a wedding at Cana in Galilee. The mother of Jesus was there, <sup>2</sup> and Jesus and his disciples had also been invited. <sup>3</sup> When they ran out of wine, since the wine provided for the wedding was all finished, the mother <sup>4</sup> of Jesus said to him, "They have no wine." ·Jesus said, "Woman, why turn to me? My hour has not <sup>5</sup> come yet." ·His mother said to the servants, "Do <sup>6</sup> whatever he tells you." ·There were six stone water jars standing there, meant for the ablutions that are customary among the Jews: each could <sup>7</sup> hold twenty or thirty gallons. ·Jesus said to the servants, "Fill the jars with water," and they filled <sup>8</sup> them to the brim. ·"Draw some out now," he told <sup>9</sup> them, "and take it to the steward." ·They did this; the steward tasted the water, and it had turned into wine. Having no idea where it came from—only the servants who had drawn the water knew—<sup>10</sup> the steward called the bridegroom ·and said, "People generally serve the best wine first, and keep the cheaper sort till the guests have had plenty to drink; but you have kept the best wine till now."

<sup>11</sup> This was the first of the signs given by Jesus: it was given at Cana in Galilee. He let his glory be

12 seen, and his disciples believed in him. •After this
he went down to Capernaum with his mother and
brothers, but they stayed there only a few days.

✠

In presenting Jesus in action for the first time, John
gives us a number of clues about how to understand the
story. In 2:11 he calls this incident a sign, which in his
vocabulary does not simply mean a miracle, as in the
traditional phrase "signs and portents" (4:48), but indicates that one must perceive the meaning of the event
in order to understand it. Signs always point beyond
themselves. In the same verse he indicates that Jesus
"let his glory be seen," and in response the disciples
"believed in him." Thus the sign is not merely a miracle to arouse astonishment but a manifestation of the
divine glory. It is only when a miracle story can be seen
this way, as a kind of epiphany of the divine, that it
can arouse faith—in the characters in the Gospel or in
the readers of it.

There are other clues also. The story itself, on the
level of simple narrative, leaves too many questions
unanswered, and the setting is implausible. Jesus refers
to his "hour," which in the special vocabulary of the
Fourth Gospel means the passion-resurrection. It has
not come yet but is apparently anticipated here. In this
light perhaps we should translate the opening words
literally "on the third day" and allow the inevitable
connotation of the resurrection to stand. In this Gospel
it is precisely the death and resurrection of Jesus which
is the ultimate manifestation of Jesus' divine glory, and

that is somehow to be seen as anticipated in the miracle
of changing water to wine at Cana. The only other appearance of Jesus' mother in the Gospel (19:25-27)
links this story with the passion.

We are thus led by the evangelist to read this story
on a symbolic level and not merely on a story level.
The trouble is that there are so many symbolic allusions in it. For example, contemporaries of the Gospel
in the Greco-Roman world would be quite familiar
with the manifestation of the god Dionysus in worship
and even in miracles involving wine. Whether that
background is relevant here or not is uncertain. There
may also be in the mention of the ablution jars an allusion to the inadequacy of Jewish ritual to cope with
real human need. But the most plausible area of symbolism—in addition to the reference to the passion—is
that of the messianic setting in which the identity of
Jesus as Messiah is implied. The occasion is a wedding
feast, which, as the parables in Matthew 22:1-14
show, was a messianic occasion. The great abundance
of wine provided recalls the imagery of Amos 9:13-14.
Most of all, the remark of the steward in verse 10,
"You have kept the best wine till now," invites the conclusion that the Messiah is now here.

Jesus' moving to Capernaum as the center of his
Galilean ministry is part of the tradition (see Mk 1:21;
2:1), but John has no interest in keeping him there.
Hence the rather abrupt statement that he didn't stay
long. The remainder of the Book of Signs shows Jesus
constantly traveling to and from Jerusalem. Unlike the
synoptic evangelists, John does not confine Jesus' ministry to a single year.

STUDY QUESTIONS: To what extent is an understanding
of the Old Testament and its
themes a part of the Christian message? What difference does it make
to the Christian follower of Jesus?

## John 2:13–22
## ZEAL FOR YOUR HOUSE

<sup>13</sup> Just before the Jewish Passover Jesus went up
<sup>14</sup> to Jerusalem, ·and in the Temple he found people
selling cattle and sheep and pigeons, and the
moneychangers sitting at their counters there.
<sup>15</sup> Making a whip out of some cord, he drove them
all out of the Temple, cattle and sheep as well,
scattered the moneychangers' coins, knocked their
<sup>16</sup> tables over ·and said to the pigeon sellers, "Take
all this out of here and stop turning my Father's
<sup>17</sup> house into a market." ·Then his disciples remem-
bered the words of scripture: Zeal for your house
<sup>18</sup> will devour me. ·The Jews intervened and said,
"What sign can you show us to justify what you
<sup>19</sup> have done?" ·Jesus answered, "Destroy this sanc-
<sup>20</sup> tuary, and in three days I will raise it up." ·The
Jews replied, "It has taken forty-six years to build
this sanctuary: are you going to raise it up in three
<sup>21</sup> days?" ·But he was speaking of the sanctuary that
<sup>22</sup> was his body, ·and when Jesus rose from the dead,
his disciples remembered that he had said this,
and they believed the scripture and the words he
had said.

✠

John tells the story of the cleansing of the Temple near the beginning of Jesus' ministry; the synoptic writers connect it with the passion narrative (see, e.g., Mk 11:15–19). But we must remember that they had no choice, since for them Jesus visited Jerusalem only once. It is completely unlikely that Jesus might have performed this prophetic gesture twice, and we have no sure way of deciding between John and the other Gospels about the timing of it. For John it establishes the prophetic role of Jesus at the outset and furnishes an opportunity to have him mention his Father for the first time.

The evangelist is still a reinterpreter here. He combines the traditional story with a saying of Jesus about destroying the Temple (see Mk 14:58) and with a challenge to Jesus' authority to exercise a prophetic role (see Mk 11:28). The Jews demand a sign—the word is used here in the sense of a proof of authority— as in other contexts they do in the synoptic tradition (e.g., Mk 8:11–12). If they are meant to understand Jesus as acting like a prophet, their demand for a sign is the classic test of a prophet (see Dt 13:2–3 [= 13:1–2]). This scene in the synoptic tradition is connected with quotations from Isaiah 56:7 and Jeremiah 7:11. John has felt free to cite Psalm 69:9.

The variation in Old Testament passages is an important reminder of how the early Christians turned to their Bible and reinterpreted it in terms of their experience of Jesus and their traditions about him. This procedure is explicitly referred to in verse 22 (and in 12:16, which is a very close parallel). The statement is important for understanding John and indeed all the Gospels. They are all written from the post-Easter perspective of the Christian churches and in the light of

Old Testament reinterpretation. John calls this process
"remembering," which means something closer to theological reflection than merely recalling. The warrant for
this creative activity on the part of evangelists and
others is the work of the Paraclete, or Advocate, the
Holy Spirit in the community, who will "remind" (literally "cause to remember") the disciples of all that
Jesus has said (14:26). It is the same awareness of the
Spirit that authorizes the Johannine church to rein-
terpret the tradition in its own distinctive way.

STUDY QUESTION: Do we approach the Gospels mainly
                to learn "the facts" about Jesus, or
                to learn what he means for the lives
                of his followers?

## John 2:23 to 3:21
## GOD LOVED THE WORLD SO MUCH

23 During his stay in Jerusalem for the Passover
many believed in his name when they saw the
24 signs that he gave, ·but Jesus knew them all and
25 did not trust himself to them; ·he never needed
evidence about any man; he could tell what a man
had in him.

1 3 There was one of the Pharisees called Nico-
2 demus, a leading Jew, ·who came to Jesus by
night and said, "Rabbi, we know that you are a
teacher who comes from God; for no one could
perform the signs that you do unless God were
3 with him." ·Jesus answered:

"I tell you most solemnly,
unless a man is born from above,
he cannot see the kingdom of God."

4 Nicodemus said, "How can a grown man be born?
Can he go back into his mother's womb and be
5 born again?" ·Jesus replied:

"I tell you most solemnly,
unless a man is born through water and the
Spirit,
he cannot enter the kingdom of God:
6 what is born of the flesh is flesh;
what is born of the Spirit is spirit.

7 Do not be surprised when I say:
  You must be born from above.
8 The wind blows wherever it pleases;
  you hear its sound,
      but you cannot tell where it comes from or
          where it is going.
  That is how it is with all who are born of the
      Spirit."

9 "How can that be possible?" asked Nicodemus.
10 "You, a teacher in Israel, and you do not know
   these things!" replied Jesus.

11 "I tell you most solemnly,
   we speak only about what we know
   and witness only to what we have seen
   and yet you people reject our evidence.
12 If you do not believe me
   when I speak about things in this world,
   how are you going to believe me
   when I speak to you about heavenly things?
13 No one has gone up to heaven
   except the one who came down from heaven,
   the Son of Man who is in heaven;
14 and the Son of Man must be lifted up
   as Moses lifted up the serpent in the desert,
15 so that everyone who believes may have eternal
       life in him.
16 Yes, God loved the world so much
   that he gave his only Son,
   so that everyone who believes in him may not
       be lost
   but may have eternal life.
17 For God sent his Son into the world
   not to condemn the world,
   but so that through him the world might be
       saved.
18 No one who believes in him will be condemned;
   but whoever refuses to believe is condemned
       already,
   because he has refused to believe
   in the name of God's only Son.

19    On these grounds is sentence pronounced:
      that though the light has come into the world
      men have shown they prefer
      darkness to the light
      because their deeds were evil.
20    And indeed, everybody who does wrong
      hates the light and avoids it,
      for fear his actions should be exposed;
21    but the man who lives by the truth
      comes out into the light,
      so that it may be plainly seen that what he does
         is done in God."


✠


The final verses of chapter 2 serve better an an introduction to what follows than a conclusion to the Temple story. They contain a sharp criticism of faith that is based merely on seeing the miracles of Jesus. In the Greek of verses 23–24 there is a play on words which we might paraphrase: "many *believed* in his name when they saw the signs that he gave, but Jesus knew them all and did not let himself be *believed* in by them." True faith comes from seeing God's revelation in Jesus, and though that can be seen in the signs if they are understood properly, it comes primarily through Jesus' revealing word. Thus the ambiguity of Nicodemus. He comes to Jesus secretly with a faith, or at least a curiosity, based on signs alone, but he does not seem able to accept the revealing word with which Jesus challenges him.

Actually, the reader doesn't know how Nicodemus turns out. When we meet him again in discussions among Jews (7:50–52) and at the burial of Jesus (19:39, both passages with typical Johannine cross ref-

erences), we don't know whether he has come fully to
be a believer or whether he represents the class of cryptobelievers who are afraid to confess their faith openly
(see 12:42–43). But John is not so much interested in
the personal history of Nicodemus as in the opportunity
to introduce the word of Jesus in action and to present
the first of many discourses of Jesus.

The dialogue with Nicodemus, which remains unre-
solved, is a good example of a favorite technique of this
Gospel. Jesus' revealing word is often, because of the
very simplicity of his language, ambiguous, and more
often than not it provokes misunderstanding. Jesus demands that the would-be believer must undergo a spiritual birth, enter on a new life, which the Gospel calls
"eternal life," in which the person is turned toward
God and is receptive to God's revelation. But he states
this in a phrase which in Greek means both "born from
above" and "born again." Strictly speaking, Jesus could
mean either one here, though "born from above" better
fits the thought of the Fourth Gospel. But Nicodemus is
not open to the symbolic meaning and stays at the level
of incredulity about being born a second time.

The Christian tradition has often understood this
passage to refer to baptism, but it is not certain that
John intended such a reference. Even the phrase "born
through water and the Spirit" (3:5) may be using two
words for the same thing, since water symbolizes the
Spirit in John (see 7:37–39). This Gospel is not unaware of sacramental practice but places very little emphasis on it.

Starting with verse 11, Jesus moves into a discourse
and addresses a plural "you." This beautiful and rightly
loved passage is typical of the discourses in the Gospel.
It emphasizes such Johannine themes as the contrast

between the heavenly and the earthly, between light and darkness, eternal life, truth, and the function of Jesus' words as provoking judgment (in the JB such terms as "condemn" and "pronouncing sentence" are used). The judgment which the individual undergoes is for or against Jesus; there is no middle ground.

Since there were no quotation marks in ancient copies of the Gospel, we are unsure whether verses 11–21 are all meant to be spoken by Jesus or whether verses 16–21 are the evangelist's own reflection. The dilemma is instructive, however, for it reminds us that the discourses placed on the lips of Jesus in this Gospel are in the evangelist's own style and they embody his theological reflections on the meaning of Jesus for his people.

Verse 14 contains a remarkably bold allusion to the Old Testament that is found also in some other ancient Jewish and Christian literature. The story is told in Numbers 21:4–9 of how Moses, on Yahweh's instruction, placed a bronze serpent on a pole to save the lives of those afflicted with fatal snake bites. John uses this vivid image to refer to Jesus' death on the cross, which is a source of eternal life for believers. The three references to the lifting up of the Son of Man in John (3:14; 8:28; 12:32–34) are the Johannine counterpart to the three predictions of the passion, also in terms of the Son of Man, in the synoptic tradition (see Mk 8:31; 9:31; 10:33–34).

STUDY QUESTION: What are the conditions for arriving at true Christian faith?

# John 3:22–36
## THE BRIDEGROOM'S FRIEND

²² After this, Jesus went with his disciples into the Judaean countryside and stayed with them there ²³ and baptized. ·At the same time John was baptizing at Aenon near Salim, where there was plenty of water, and people were going there to ²⁴ be baptized. ·This was before John had been put in prison.

²⁵ Now some of John's disciples had opened a ²⁶ discussion with a Jew about purification, ·so they went to John and said, "Rabbi, the man who was with you on the far side of the Jordan, the man to whom you bore witness, is baptizing now; and ²⁷ everyone is going to him." ·John replied:

"A man can lay claim
only to what is given him from heaven.

²⁸ "You yourselves can bear me out: I said: I myself am not the Christ; I am the one who has been sent in front of him.

²⁹ "The bride is only for the bridegroom;
and yet the bridegroom's friend,
who stands there and listens,
is glad when he hears the bridegroom's voice.
This same joy I feel, and now it is complete.

30    He must grow greater,
        I must grow smaller.
31    He who comes from above
        is above all others;
        he who is born of the earth
        is earthly himself and speaks in an earthly way.
        He who comes from heaven
32    bears witness to the things he has seen and
          heard,
        even if his testimony is not accepted;
33    though all who do accept his testimony
        are attesting the truthfulness of God,
34    since he whom God has sent
        speaks God's own words:
        God gives him the Spirit without reserve.
35    The Father loves the Son
        and has entrusted everything to him.
36    Anyone who believes in the Son has eternal life,
        but anyone who refuses to believe in the Son
          will never see life:
        the anger of God stays on him."

☩

John the Baptist reappears in the Gospel, and again it is to bear witness to Jesus by contrasting his own role as a mere forerunner or herald with that of Jesus as the Messiah. The other Gospels give us no hint that Jesus was once a baptizer like John, and there must have been some discussion of this issue in the community of the Fourth Gospel, since 4:2 places a qualification on 3:22 by confining the baptizing to Jesus' disciples. Perhaps the "correction" is evidence of the stages of composition in John.

From verse 31 on we have the same dilemma we had

in the last passage. Who is the speaker? Since no one else is mentioned, the JB assumes it is the Baptist who goes on speaking. Yet the verses sound very much like the discourse of Jesus earlier in the chapter—or like the evangelist's reflections. In the complex and probably long process in which the Gospel took shape, this section might have been part of a discourse of Jesus related to 3:11–21. It may be thought appropriate here because it picks up the theme of witnessing, but now it is Jesus who witnesses to the Father.

The radical separation between "above" and "the earth," which some have called Johannine dualism, is expressed in this discourse in strong terms. Only Jesus has bridged the gap, for he is the one who came from heaven to speak God's own words in the world. The consistent pattern of John's Christology is that of the descent and eventual reascent of Jesus; often (as in 3:13) this pattern is particularly associated with the title Son of Man. By speaking God's words in the world, however, that is, by creating faith and conferring eternal life, the Johannine Jesus makes it possible for Christians also to bridge the gap between "above" and "below." The dualism is overcome by faith because Jesus has overcome it in the incarnation.

STUDY QUESTIONS: Does the attitude of John the Baptist suggest any model for the Christian's relationship to Jesus? How does a particular understanding of who Jesus is affect the way a believer behaves?

# John 4:1–42
## GIVE ME SOME OF THAT WATER

¹ 4 When Jesus heard that the Pharisees had found out that he was making and baptizing ² more disciples than John—•though in fact it was ³ his disciples who baptized, not Jesus himself—•he ⁴ left Judaea and went back to Galilee. •This meant that he had to cross Samaria.

⁵ On the way he came to the Samaritan town called Sychar, near the land that Jacob gave to ⁶ his son Joseph. •Jacob's well is there and Jesus, tired by the journey, sat straight down by the well. ⁷ It was about the sixth hour. •When a Samaritan woman came to draw water, Jesus said to her, ⁸ "Give me a drink." •His disciples had gone into ⁹ the town to buy food. •The Samaritan woman said to him, "What? You are a Jew and you ask me, a Samaritan, for a drink?"—Jews, in fact, do not ¹⁰ associate with Samaritans. •Jesus replied:

> "If you only knew what God is offering
> and who it is that is saying to you:
> Give me a drink,
> you would have been the one to ask,
> and he would have given you living water."

¹¹ "You have no bucket, sir," she answered, "and the well is deep: how could you get this living

¹² water? ·Are you a greater man than our father
Jacob who gave us this well and drank from it
¹³ himself with his sons and his cattle?" ·Jesus replied:

> "Whoever drinks this water
> will get thirsty again;
¹⁴     but anyone who drinks the water that I shall
> give
> will never be thirsty again:
> the water that I shall give
> will turn into a spring inside him, welling up
> to eternal life."

¹⁵   "Sir," said the woman, "give me some of that
water, so that I may never get thirsty and never
¹⁶ have to come here again to draw water." ·"Go
and call your husband," said Jesus to her, "and
¹⁷ come back here." ·The woman answered, "I have
no husband." He said to her, "You are right to
¹⁸ say, 'I have no husband'; ·for although you have
had five, the one you have now is not your hus-
¹⁹ band. You spoke the truth there." ·"I see you are
²⁰ a prophet, sir," said the woman. ·"Our fathers
worshiped on this mountain, while you say that
Jerusalem is the place where one ought to wor-
²¹ ship." ·Jesus said:

> "Believe me, woman, the hour is coming
> when you will worship the Father
> neither on this mountain nor in Jerusalem.
²²     You worship what you do not know;
> we worship what we do know;
> for salvation comes from the Jews.
²³     But the hour will come—in fact it is here al-
> ready—
> when true worshipers will worship the Father
> in spirit and truth:
> that is the kind of worshiper
> the Father wants.

24      God is spirit,
        and those who worship
        must worship in spirit and truth."

25      The woman said to him, "I know that Messiah
        —that is, Christ—is coming; and when he comes
26      he will tell us everything." ·"I who am speaking
        to you," said Jesus, "I am he."

27      At this point his disciples returned, and were
        surprised to find him speaking to a woman, though
        none of them asked, "What do you want from
28      her?" or, "Why are you talking to her?" ·The
        woman put down her water jar and hurried back
29      to the town to tell the people, ·"Come and see a
        man who has told me everything I ever did; I
30      wonder if he is the Christ?" ·This brought people
        out of the town and they started walking toward
        him.

31      Meanwhile, the disciples were urging him,
32      "Rabbi, do have something to eat"; ·but he said,
        "I have food to eat that you do not know about."
33      So the disciples asked one another, "Has someone
34      been bringing him food?" ·But Jesus said:

        "My food
        is to do the will of the one who sent me,
        and to complete his work.
35      Have you not got a saying:
        Four months and then the harvest?
        Well, I tell you:
        Look around you, look at the fields;
        already they are white, ready for harvest!
36      Already ·the reaper is being paid his wages,
        already he is bringing in the grain for eternal
            life,
        and thus sower and reaper rejoice together.
37      For here the proverb holds good:
        one sows, another reaps;
38      I sent you to reap
        a harvest you had not worked for.

Others worked for it;
and you have come into the rewards of their
    trouble."

89    Many Samaritans of that town had believed in
      him on the strength of the woman's testimony
      when she said, "He told me all I have ever done,"
40    so, when the Samaritans came up to him, they
      begged him to stay with them. He stayed for two
41    days, and ·when he spoke to them many more
42    came to believe; ·and they said to the woman,
      "Now we no longer believe because of what you
      told us; we have heard him ourselves and we
      know that he really is the savior of the world."


                              ☩


Because the Fourth Gospel is a more conscious literary reinterpretation than the other Gospels, it does not
always lend itself to division into short passages. It will
often be the case that we must comment on long sections. But in the beloved story of the woman at the
well the evangelist has practiced some of his skillful
dramatic techniques, particularly in the way he sand-
wiches the scene with the disciples between the departure of the woman and the arrival of her fellow
townspeople. It is relatively easy, therefore, to organize
our comments around the successive scenes of the
drama.

SCENE 1: verses 5–26. Jesus' encounter with the
Samaritan woman, which takes the form of a dialogue,
is clearly divided into two parts, distinguished both
by theme and by style. The first (verses 7–15) begins with Jesus asking for water and ends with the

JOHN 4:1–42 65

woman making a similar request. But in between lies a
superb example of Johannine ambiguity and misunderstanding. The symbol in question is that of "living
water," which can be understood on a natural level as
fresh, running water, but symbolically it represents
God's gift that comes through Jesus—revelation, the
Holy Spirit, eternal life. There is no reason to think the
woman understands the symbol any better than Nicodemus did the birth from above, but she remains open
to Jesus' word even when she doesn't understand.

In response to the woman's continued interest, Jesus
challenges her with a personal word that calls into
question her moral life (second part, verses 16–26).
Her response is a classic evasion—a theological discussion of the conflict between Samaritans and Jews over
the proper place of worship. Jesus transcends the issue
with a short discourse on true worship of the Father.
Two things may be singled out from this part of the
scene. First, given the obvious antipathy of the Fourth
Gospel toward "the Jews," which we shall discuss further below, it is surprising to hear Jesus say "salvation
comes from the Jews." Yet that is precisely the point:
Jesus is a Jew and so are his early followers. The very
poignancy of Johannine opposition to "the Jews" arises
out of the breach that has arisen between the Johannine church and its Jewish origin. This situation helps
to explain the favorable portrayal of willing acceptance
of faith in Jesus on the part of the traditional enemies
of the Jews, the Samaritans. The enmity is the sharper
because the two groups share much in common.

The second point is the progression of christological
titles. The woman first acknowledges Jesus as a prophet
(4:19) and then, in response to Jesus' own self-revela-
tion, as the Messiah (verses 25–26 and 29). But in

both cases her faith is based on his extraordinary insight into her life—the equivalent of a "sign." It is only when the townspeople respond to his word that these christological categories are superseded.

**SCENE 2: verses 27–38.** The brief discourse of Jesus to the disciples in verses 34–38 is at first sight difficult to understand. The important thing is to be aware that, like many passages in the Gospel, it fuses the two levels of meaning essential to the story: the "historical" level of Jesus and his disciples and the contemporary level of the Christian community of the Gospel. The disciples, representing the community leaders of the evangelist's time, are being invited to share in the work of preaching the gospel, of confronting people with the revealing word of Jesus—and thus of doing the Father's will. Thus the two proverbs cited are given a new interpretation. In the Fourth Gospel itself the time between the sowing and the harvest has been collapsed (verse 35) and the reaper and sower of the Christian mission (verse 37) rejoice together. This indirect commissioning of the followers of Jesus to carry on his work gets its force from its position within the drama of the Samaritans' faith.

**SCENE 3: verses 39–42.** If the woman's faith had been based on Jesus' sign-activity as prophet with divine insight, it is made explicit here that the people go beyond that with a faith-response to his word (JB translates "when he spoke to them," verse 41). And in accordance with the degrees of faith reflected in the titles predicated of Jesus, the townspeople go beyond "prophet" and "Messiah" to acknowledge Jesus as "savior of the world."

The apparent success of Jesus' encounter with the Samaritans stands out in the Book of Signs. In almost all his encounters with Jews from Galilee to the north or Judaea to the south, he meets with opposition to some degree. One can speculate whether the favorable response of Samaritans rests on a historical role of Samaritans in early Christianity, but the evidence is too slight to be conclusive. What is more important in this carefully wrought story is the dynamic of coming to faith in response to Jesus' word—and the mission of Jesus' disciples to continue the process.

STUDY QUESTIONS: How does the reaction of the woman at the well differ from that of Nicodemus? What is implied for Christians in Jesus' instruction to the disciples?

## John 4:43–54
## YOUR SON WILL LIVE

43 When the two days were over Jesus left for
44 Galilee. ·He himself had declared that there is no
45 respect for a prophet in his own country, ·but on
his arrival the Galileans received him well, having seen all that he had done at Jerusalem during
the festival which they too had attended.

46 He went again to Cana in Galilee, where he
had changed the water into wine. Now there was
a court official there whose son was ill at Caper-
47 naum ·and, hearing that Jesus had arrived in Galilee from Judaea, he went and asked him to come
and cure his son as he was at the point of death.
48 Jesus said, "So you will not believe unless you see
49 signs and portents!" ·"Sir," answered the official,
50 "come down before my child dies." ·"Go home,"
said Jesus, "your son will live." The man believed
51 what Jesus had said and started on his way; ·and
while he was still on the journey back his servants
52 met him with the news that his boy was alive. ·He
asked them when the boy had begun to recover.
"The fever left him yesterday," they said, "at the
53 seventh hour." ·The father realized that this was
exactly the time when Jesus had said, "Your son
will live"; and he and all his household believed.
54 This was the second sign given by Jesus, on
his return from Judaea to Galilee.

☩

The second sign at Cana in Galilee, which may have
stood second in a hypothetical "signs source" used by
the evangelist, continues the issue of faith as response
to signs or to word. Again both are present. The traditional story which John reinterprets is attested in the
source common to Matthew and Luke (see Mt 8:5–13
and Lk 7:1–10). There the focus is not so much on the
miracle of healing at a distance but on the faith of the
gentiles as contrasted with the rejection of Jesus by
Jews. In the reinterpretation in John, nothing of the
Jew-gentile issue remains.

Instead, the clue to the story lies in verse 48, which
is clearly a Johannine insertion, both because it inter-
rupts the narrative and because it is spoken to a plural
"you," not just to the court official. The tone is one of
mild frustration, as the translation indicates, and the
statement should be compared with the criticism of
signs-faith in 2:23–25. Because the situation is so appropriate, Jesus can respond to his petitioner with only
a word, but verse 50 makes it explicit that the man
believed on the basis of the word. In this instance the
miracle, carefully attested in verses 51–53, serves to
confirm the power of Jesus' word. Jesus manifests himself as the one who gives life. Belief in the signs of this
life-giving power is inadequate only when it focuses on
the signs alone and not on the revealing person of their
author.

STUDY QUESTION: Why is the Gospel of John critical of
                faith based on miracles?

# John 5:1–18
## MY FATHER GOES ON WORKING

1 5 Some time after this there was a Jewish fes-
2  tival, and Jesus went up to Jerusalem. ·Now
at the Sheep Pool in Jerusalem there is a building,
called Bethzatha in Hebrew, consisting of five
3 porticoes; ·and under these were crowds of sick
people—blind, lame, paralyzed—waiting for the
4 water to move; ·for at intervals the angel of the
Lord came down into the pool, and the water was
disturbed, and the first person to enter the water
after this disturbance was cured of any ailment he
5 suffered from. ·One man there had an illness
6 which had lasted thirty-eight years, ·and when
Jesus saw him lying there and knew he had been
in this condition for a long time, he said, "Do you
7 want to be well again?" ·"Sir," replied the sick
man, "I have no one to put me into the pool when
the water is disturbed; and while I am still on the
8 way, someone else gets there before me." ·Jesus
said, "Get up, pick up your sleeping mat and
9 walk." ·The man was cured at once, and he picked
up his mat and walked away.

10  Now that day happened to be the sabbath, ·so
the Jews said to the man who had been cured,
"It is the sabbath; you are not allowed to carry
11 your sleeping mat." ·He replied, "But the man
who cured me told me, 'Pick up your mat and

¹² walk.'" ·They asked, "Who is the man who said
¹³ to you, 'Pick up your mat and walk?'" ·The man
    had no idea who it was, since Jesus had disap-
¹⁴ peared into the crowd that filled the place. ·After
    a while Jesus met him in the Temple and said,
    "Now you are well again, be sure not to sin any
    more, or something worse may happen to you."
¹⁵ The man went back and told the Jews that it was
¹⁶ Jesus who had cured him. ·It was because he did
    things like this on the sabbath that the Jews be-
¹⁷ gan to persecute Jesus. ·His answer to them was,
¹⁸ "My Father goes on working, and so do I." ·But
    that only made the Jews even more intent on
    killing him, because, not content with breaking
    the sabbath, he spoke of God as his own Father,
    and so made himself God's equal.

☩

    In the Introduction to this commentary we discussed
the possibility that there are dislocations of passages in
the Gospel as we have it. Most of them are hazardous
for the commentator, but there is good reason to suggest that chapters 5 and 6 are in the wrong order. The
main reason is not so much that transposing these two
chapters would straighten out the geographical movements of Jesus between Galilee and Jerusalem. It
would of course help, but not completely. More impor-
tantly, if chapter 6 followed chapter 4, it would conclude the main issue of signs, words, and faith; and
chapters 5, 7, and the following would address a new
issue: the challenge of Jesus' revealing word to the religious institutions of establishment Judaism. There are
also internal reasons to think chapter 7 was meant to

follow chapter 5 (see 7:23, the issue of the sabbath).
Since even modern Bibles do not venture to transpose
chapters, we shall deal with them in their traditional
order.

Though the "Jewish festival" (5:1) cannot be identified with certainty—in contrast to the specifically
identified feasts of Passover, Tabernacles, and Dedication in other chapters—the issue hinges, somewhat
superficially, on the traditional point of sabbath violation. The gospel tradition has stories of Jesus healing a
paralyzed man (e.g., Mk 2:1–12), and it may be one
of these that John is reinterpreting here. But there are
only minimal literary contacts with the synoptic tradition.

The setting of this healing miracle—which is not
called a sign, unless perhaps it is referred to in
7:31—has fascinated students of the Gospel. Archae-
ological investigations in Jerusalem have turned up a
double pool with five colonnades ("porticoes")—four
forming a rectangle, with one running through the middle. And the cryptic Copper Scroll from among the
Dead Sea Scrolls has authenticated the name of a pool
in Jerusalem as Bethesda (rather than Bethzatha, as JB
reads). But this setting may have been that of a pagan
shrine to the popular healing god Asclepius. At a later
time the pool was certainly that, and such a situation is
not impossible in first-century Jerusalem. Actually it
helps to explain the fact that verses 3b–4, "waiting for
the water to move . . . any ailment he suffered from,"
look like an attempt to bring a pagan shrine within the
Jewish ambit by introducing an angel of the Lord.
These verses are almost certainly not part of the original text.

The issue of a violation of sabbath laws against work

is somewhat artificial to the story. It serves to stimulate conflict with "the Jews," and it is clear that the miracle itself serves mainly to provide an occasion for a conflict discourse of Jesus. What is most surprising is the abrupt way in which the Jewish resolve to put Jesus to death enters the Gospel. Recall that the reader is expected to know the story and thus not to need a plausible motivation for all the issues raised.

By this time in John "the Jews" are recognized as totally hostile to Jesus, and we must say a word about this term. The Fourth Gospel is not, strictly speaking, anti-Jewish, much less anti-Semitic, though unhappily it may have contributed to Christian anti-Semitism in history. It is not anti-Jewish in any general sense because its opposition to "the Jews," which indeed becomes very fierce in the discourse of chapter 8 and in the passion narrative, reflects the Johannine church's resentment against forced separation from its own background in a Jewish community (see 9:22; 12:42; 16:2). The term "the Jews" is generally equivalent to "the Pharisees," who were the sole leaders of the Jewish communities when the Gospel was written.

STUDY QUESTION: What is the relationship between religious "laws," like the sabbath law, and faith in the Messiah Jesus?

# John 5:19–47
## THE SON GIVES LIFE
## TO ANYONE HE CHOOSES

19 To this accusation Jesus replied:

"I tell you most solemnly,
the Son can do nothing by himself;
he can do only what he sees the Father doing:
and whatever the Father does the Son does too.
20 For the Father loves the Son
and shows him everything he does himself,
and he will show him even greater things than
    these,
works that will astonish you.
21 Thus, as the Father raises the dead and gives
    them life,
so the Son gives life to anyone he chooses;
22 for the Father judges no one;
he has entrusted all judgment to the Son,
23 so that all may honor the Son
as they honor the Father.
Whoever refuses honor to the Son
refuses honor to the Father who sent him.
24 I tell you most solemnly,
whoever listens to my words,
and believes in the one who sent me,
has eternal life;

without being brought to judgment
he has passed from death to life.

25 I tell you most solemnly,
the hour will come—in fact it is here already—
when the dead will hear the voice of the Son of
    God,
and all who hear it will live.

26 For the Father, who is the source of life,
has made the Son the source of life;

27 and, because he is the Son of Man,
has appointed him supreme judge.

28 Do not be surprised at this,
for the hour is coming
when the dead will leave their graves
at the sound of his voice:

29 those who did good
will rise again to life;
and those who did evil, to condemnation.

30 I can do nothing by myself;
I can only judge as I am told to judge,
and my judging is just,
because my aim is to do not my own will,
but the will of him who sent me.

31 "Were I to testify on my own behalf,
my testimony would not be valid;

32 but there is another witness who can speak on
    my behalf,
and I know that his testimony is valid.

33 You sent messengers to John,
and he gave his testimony to the truth:

34 not that I depend on human testimony;
no, it is for your salvation that I speak of this.

35 John was a lamp alight and shining
and for a time you were content to enjoy the
    light that he gave.

36 But my testimony is greater than John's:
the works my Father has given me to carry out,
these same works of mine
testify that the Father has sent me.

37    Besides, the Father who sent me
      bears witness to me himself.
      You have never heard his voice,
      you have never seen his shape,
38    and his word finds no home in you
      because you do not believe
      in the one he has sent.

39    "You study the scriptures,
      believing that in them you have eternal life;
      now these same scriptures testify to me,
40    and yet you refuse to come to me for life!
41    As for human approval, this means nothing to
           me.
42    Besides, I know you too well:
      you have no love of God in you.
43    I have come in the name of my Father
      and you refuse to accept me;
      if someone else comes in his own name
      you will accept him.
44    How can you believe,
      since you look to one another for approval
      and are not concerned
      with the approval that comes from the one
           God?
45    Do not imagine that I am going to accuse you
           before the Father:
      you place your hopes on Moses,
      and Moses will be your accuser.
46    If you really believed him
      you would believe me too,
      since it was I that he was writing about;
47    but if you refuse to believe what he wrote,
      how can you believe what I say?"

                          ✠

The controversy occasioned by the "giving of life" to the paralytic leads into a long discourse of Jesus that increases tension in its challenge to the Jews. Along the way it develops a number of the typical themes of the discourses in the Fourth Gospel. Like most of these discourses, it is highly repetitive, but powerful in its impact as revealing and challenging word. It is closely linked with its context. The Jews had challenged Jesus' authority to act as he did, and he defended it with an appeal to his Father's activity (5:17). The discourse elaborates on this defense.

In the first section, verses 19–30, Jesus explains the relationship of what he does—that is, how his word functions to provoke judgment—to what the Father does and commissions him to do. Here we meet a trait of the Gospel that occurs in several discourses and sayings of Jesus. It is the placing side by side of basically different perspectives on time and the future, that is, on eschatology. The first part of the section, up to verse 25, which is transitional, refers to the believer possessing eternal life in the present, having already met judgment in hearing Jesus' word. Such a person has already "passed from death to life." This perspective, which is often called realized eschatology, is characteristic of the Gospel of John and occurs throughout. The rest of the section takes up the same theme of Jesus' role, but this time against the background of more traditional, future eschatology which looks to death, judgment, and resurrection in the future. It is possible that the evangelist means to include both perspectives and to assert that Jesus is the focal point of both of them. Many interpreters, however, prefer to see them as evidence of dis-

cussion on the subject of eschatology within the Johannine church. Since the Gospel is in other respects the
result of a complex process of composition, it may include various stages of theological speculation.

The remainder of the discourse, from verse 31 on-
ward, reintroduces the theme of witness to Jesus and
develops it quite systematically. The problem is one of
Jewish law: If Jesus bears witness to himself—as he certainly appears to do—his witness is legally invalid.
Hence he appeals to a succession of witnesses that cor-
roborate his authority. The list is impressive and very
revealing of Johannine theology.

The first witness cited is again John the Baptist
(5:31–35), who is spoken of warmly—"a lamp alight
and shining"—but still kept in his subordinate place.
The second witness is "the works" of Jesus. On the
surface this phrase is Jesus' own description of his miracles or "signs." Yet, as will become clearer in succeed-
ing chapters, Jesus' works are the "work" of the Father
—singular and plural of key terms like "work," "sin,"
"commandment" seem to be interchangeable. And the
work of the Father is bringing people to faith. God
himself, the Father, is cited as the third witness to Jesus
(verse 37). Some think God's witness is merely an introduction to the fourth, the scriptures in which the
voice of God is heard, but this point is at least not
explicitly made. Since Jesus reveals the Father in himself, God's witness is heard in all he says and does. The
scriptures are a witness to Jesus in the sense that the
early Christians appealed to them to articulate their
faith (see the commentary on 2:22). In typical Johannine irony, the scriptural appeal is effective in the argu-

ment with the Jews, because the Bible is their own authority par excellence.

STUDY QUESTION: What are the effective witnesses to Christ in contemporary Christian experience?

# John 6:1–15
## THIS REALLY IS THE PROPHET

<sup>1</sup> 6 Some time after this, Jesus went off to the other side of the Sea of Galilee—or of Ti-
<sup>2</sup> berias—·and a large crowd followed him, impressed by the signs he gave by curing the sick.
<sup>3</sup> Jesus climbed the hillside, and sat down there
<sup>4</sup> with his disciples. ·It was shortly before the Jewish feast of Passover.

<sup>5</sup>   Looking up, Jesus saw the crowds approaching and said to Philip, "Where can we buy some bread
<sup>6</sup> for these people to eat?" ·He only said this to test Philip; he himself knew exactly what he was going
<sup>7</sup> to do. ·Philip answered, "Two hundred denarii would only buy enough to give them a small piece
<sup>8</sup> each." ·One of his disciples, Andrew, Simon Pe-
<sup>9</sup> ter's brother, said, ·"There is a small boy here with five barley loaves and two fish; but what
<sup>10</sup> is that between so many?" ·Jesus said to them, "Make the people sit down." There was plenty of grass there, and as many as five thousand men sat
<sup>11</sup> down. ·Then Jesus took the loaves, gave thanks, and gave them out to all who were sitting ready; he then did the same with the fish, giving out
<sup>12</sup> as much as was wanted. ·When they had eaten enough he said to the disciples, "Pick up the pieces

13 left over, so that nothing gets wasted." ·So they
picked them up, and filled twelve hampers with
scraps left over from the meal of five barley
14 loaves. ·The people, seeing this sign that he had
given, said, "This really is the prophet who is to
15 come into the world." ·Jesus, who could see they
were about to come and take him by force and
make him king, escaped back to the hills by himself.

☩

Chapter 6, which as argued above is best considered
as an immediate sequel to chapter 4, is a carefully constructed unity, even if one part of it, verses 52–59, is
an interpolation. It is possible, however, to comment on
it as a succession of smaller units because its structural
lines are clear. The overall theme is the identification of
Jesus with the bread of life or bread from heaven, and
the preoccupation of modern commentators, as well
perhaps as ancient ones, is the extent to which this
symbol is related to the eucharistic practice of the
church.

No one doubts that the popularity of the miracle of
the loaves in the early church was connected with the
eucharistic interpretation of it. It occurs twice in Mark
and Matthew and once in Luke (see Mk 6:30–44 and
8:1–9), and in all cases it contains the typical language
of the eucharistic celebration: Jesus *took* the loaves,
*blessed* them (or gave thanks), *broke* them, and *gave*
them to the disciples. The Johannine version of the
story, though it contains elements that may correspond
to the eucharistic practice of the church—for example,

the concern about picking up the pieces left over in verse 12—actually minimizes the traditional eucharistic language. Jesus *took* the loaves, *gave thanks,* and *gave them out* (that is, distributed them). The liturgical formula is broken, and Jesus' contact with the crowd is, in typical Johannine style, not mediated by the disciples.

We cannot conclude that the Fourth Gospel is not interested in the eucharistic understanding of the miracle—nor of course can we speculate on what exactly constituted the miraculous action of Jesus—but we can observe that the traditional eucharistic interpretation is not important for the evangelist. In the gift of bread Jesus gives himself, of course. Whether this gift is ritualized or not is secondary to the giving itself.

For the Fourth Gospel the christological reaction of the crowd is important. They perceive the event as a sign (verse 14) and in response to it—on a level the evangelist regards as inadequate—they proclaim Jesus to be the eschatological prophet like Moses (note the comparison with Moses in verses 31–33). Jesus sees the inadequacy of this signs-faith. Though the theme of Jesus as king is central to the Gospel, he is here portrayed as refusing to be made king.

STUDY QUESTIONS: What exactly do we celebrate in the eucharistic worship of the modern church? What gift do we receive in the bread that Jesus provides?

## John 6:16–21
## DO NOT BE AFRAID

16 That evening the disciples went down to the
17 shore of the lake and ·got into a boat to make
for Capernaum on the other side of the lake. It
was getting dark by now and Jesus had still not
18 rejoined them. ·The wind was strong, and the sea
19 was getting rough. ·They had rowed three or four
miles when they saw Jesus walking on the lake
and coming toward the boat. This frightened
20 them, ·but he said, "It is I. Do not be afraid."
21 They were for taking him into the boat, but in
no time it reached the shore at the place they
were making for.

✠

The spectacular miracle of the walking on the water
is a part of the gospel tradition which John is reinterpreting. In the synoptic tradition it is closely associated with the miracle of the loaves (see Mk
6:45–52), and here the fourth evangelist knows not
only the traditions but the sequence of them. Since he
is in most instances a creative reinterpreter, the ques-

tion here is what he intends by the inclusion of this
story on which he does not comment formally. It is idle
to try to explain away the miracle, for example by trans-
lating verse 19 "they saw Jesus walking *beside* the
lake," for the evangelist never tries to shy away from
the miraculous tradition about Jesus, even though he is
critical of it as a basis for faith.

But we must remember that when miracles are
significant for this Gospel, they are manifestations of
the divine presence in Jesus. Here the Old Testament
comes to mind in the description of God's majestic
presence to his creation in Psalm 77:19: "You strode
across the sea, you marched across the ocean, but your
steps could not be seen." Since Psalm 78 is the apparent reference in the sequel, it is not improbable that
this reference underlies the evangelist's thinking here.

Whether this is really the background of the miracle
story or not, there is another reason to regard it as a
manifestation of the divine presence in Jesus. That is
the use of the expression "It is I," literally "I am," by
Jesus at the point of recognition in the story. Some interpreters point out that several of the uses of this otherwise common expression in the Fourth Gospel reflect
the Jewish use of "I am" as a name for God (e.g., in Is
43:25 and elsewhere). We shall see even clearer examples in chapters 8 and 13. If this usage is correctly
found here, then Jesus is in a sense identifying himself
with God at the moment of his miraculous appearance.
Though it is not called a sign in the context, this miracle is a sign in the full Johannine sense.

The function of it in this somewhat complex chapter
will become clear only at the end of the chapter. It is
not directly alluded to later on. But since the disciples
represented by Peter are later on contrasted with the

larger group (see verses 67–69), perhaps we should see a contrast between the two miracles with which the episode begins. The miracle of the loaves elicits a positive response from the crowd but ultimately does not lead to faith. The miracle of the walking on the water is witnessed only by the disciples, and ultimately they confess faith in Jesus. The crowd sees the sign merely as a miracle; the disciples, implicitly perhaps, see their sign as an epiphany of the divine (see 2:11).

STUDY QUESTIONS: We may look for Jesus in moments of distress, but where do we find him? And what do we find in him?

# John 6:22–50
## I AM THE BREAD OF LIFE

<sup></sup>

22 Next day, the crowd that had stayed on the other side saw that only one boat had been there, and that Jesus had not got into the boat with his disciples, but that the disciples had set off by 23 themselves. ·Other boats, however, had put in from Tiberias, near the place where the bread had 24 been eaten. ·When the people saw that neither Jesus nor his disciples were there, they got into those boats and crossed to Capernaum to look for 25 Jesus. ·When they found him on the other side, they said to him, "Rabbi, when did you come 26 here?" ·Jesus answered:

"I tell you most solemnly,
you are not looking for me
because you have seen the signs
but because you had all the bread you wanted
    to eat.
27    Do not work for food that cannot last,
but work for food that endures to eternal life,
the kind of food the Son of Man is offering you,
for on him the Father, God himself, has set his
    seal."

28    Then they said to him, "What must we do if 29 we are to do the works that God wants?" ·Jesus gave them this answer, "This is working for God:

30 you must believe in the one he has sent." ·So they
said, "What sign will you give to show us that we
should believe in you? What work will you do?
31 Our fathers had manna to eat in the desert; as
scripture says: He gave them bread from heaven
to eat."
32     Jesus answered:

> "I tell you most solemnly,
> it was not Moses who gave you bread from
>     heaven,
> it is my Father who gives you the bread from
>     heaven,
> the true bread;
33 for the bread of God
> is that which comes down from heaven
> and gives life to the world."

34     "Sir," they said, "give us that bread always."
35 Jesus answered:

> "I am the bread of life.
> He who comes to me will never be hungry;
> he who believes in me will never thirst.
36 But, as I have told you,
> you can see me and still you do not believe.
37 All that the Father gives me will come to me,
> and whoever comes to me
> I shall not turn him away;
38 because I have come from heaven,
> not to do my own will,
> but to do the will of the one who sent me.
39 Now the will of him who sent me
> is that I should lose nothing
> of all that he has given to me,
> and that I should raise it up on the last day.
40 Yes, it is my Father's will
> that whoever sees the Son and believes in him
> shall have eternal life,
> and that I shall raise him up on the last day."

41 Meanwhile the Jews were complaining to each
other about him, because he had said, "I am the

⁴² bread that came down from heaven." ·"Surely
this is Jesus son of Joseph," they said. "We know
his father and mother. How can he now say, 'I
⁴³ have come down from heaven?'" ·Jesus said in
reply, "Stop complaining to each other.

⁴⁴      "No one can come to me
         unless he is drawn by the Father who sent me,
         and I will raise him up at the last day.
⁴⁵      It is written in the prophets:
         They will all be taught by God,
         and to hear the teaching of the Father,
         and learn from it,
         is to come to me.
⁴⁶      Not that anybody has seen the Father,
         except the one who comes from God:
         he has seen the Father.
⁴⁷      I tell you most solemnly,
         everybody who believes has eternal life.
⁴⁸      I am the bread of life.
⁴⁹      Your fathers ate the manna in the desert
         and they are dead;
⁵⁰      but this is the bread that comes down from
              heaven,
         so that a man may eat it and not die."

☩

Jesus' miraculous crossing of the lake was for the
crowds, in contrast to the disciples, merely a puzzle.
Hence the almost too detailed discussion of available
boats in verses 22–25.

Verses 26–34 serve as an introduction to the bread-
of-life discourse that follows. They contain some important clarifications of Johannine language. For example, verse 26 clearly distinguishes between seeing a sign

as such—that is, as a showing forth of the glory of God in Jesus—and seeing it merely as a miracle, in this case implying the satisfaction of having bread to eat.

In view of the importance of "the work(s) of God" in this Gospel, one should translate verses 28–29 more literally: "Then they said to him, 'What should we do in order to perform the works of God?' Jesus gave them this answer, 'This is the work of God, that you believe in the one he has sent.'" As we shall continue to observe, "doing God's work" for the Fourth Gospel is a matter of coming to faith, or bringing people to faith. The relation of "works" to "signs" is a close one, but it suggests different levels of understanding of what Jesus is doing and what his followers are to do (see, e.g., 9:4).

The background of the discourse is the story, first told in Exodus 16, of the manna sent by God to feed the Israelites in the desert. Some details of this chapter allude to this story, such as the "complaining," or "murmuring," of the people in verses 41–43, which recalls the plaintive reaction of the Israelites. The quotation in verse 31 which forms the "text" for what follows is not an exact one, but is very likely a reference to Psalm 78:24, a retelling of the Exodus story. Since the context is another demand for a sign (see 2:18), an atmosphere of antagonism is set up—the common feature of the discourses in the Book of Signs—and we are prepared for a sharp contrast to be drawn between Moses and Jesus. Jesus responds in verses 32–33 by offering a different interpretation of the verse from the psalm. The people's request for bread in verse 34 recalls the Samaritan woman's request for water in 4:15, but here the tone is different and the outcome radically in contrast.

The discourse itself, verses 35–50 (actually to verse 51a), is punctuated by Jesus' self-identification with the symbol of bread as a necessity for life (verses 35, 48, 51a). Only here the symbol is made apparent in that this bread is essential for eternal life. What is it a symbol of? The citation of Isaiah 54:13 in verse 45, which refers to divine teaching, shows that the symbol refers to revelation, as ultimately all the Johannine symbols do. Other features of this discourse are typical of the Gospel: the christological pattern of Jesus' descent from heaven and the placing side by side of different eschatological images, eternal life and resurrection on the last day.

This discourse is our first introduction to an important device of the Gospel, the use of "I am" sayings with predicates that reflect some of the common images of biblical and even extrabiblical religious language, such as bread, light, life, way, etc. The question for the reader to ask is this: Where should the emphasis lie, on the "I" or on the "bread of life"? The answer is not obvious, but it is more in harmony with the Christocentrism of the Gospel to suppose that the symbols are meant to be well known—as indeed they were in the ancient world. In that case Jesus is saying, "What you long for in the religious symbol of the bread of life is to be found in me." The emphasis is on the "I."

STUDY QUESTIONS: What does the christological symbol of bread mean to a modern Christian? How essential is faith in Christ to our lives?

## John 6:51–58
### MY FLESH IS REAL FOOD

<sup></sup>

51 "I am the living bread which has come down
      from heaven.
Anyone who eats this bread will live for ever;
and the bread that I shall give
is my flesh, for the life of the world."

52 Then the Jews started arguing with one another: "How can this man give us his flesh to
53 eat?" they said. ·Jesus replied:

"I tell you most solemnly,
if you do not eat the flesh of the Son of Man
and drink his blood,
you will not have life in you.
54 Anyone who does eat my flesh and drink my
      blood
has eternal life,
and I shall raise him up on the last day.
55 For my flesh is real food
and my blood is real drink.
56 He who eats my flesh and drinks my blood
lives in me
and I live in him.
57 As I, who am sent by the living Father,
myself draw life from the Father,
so whoever eats me will draw life from me.

58     This is the bread come down from heaven;
       not like the bread our ancestors ate:
       they are dead,
       but anyone who eats this bread will live for
       ever."


✠


There is a change of tone, and to a limited extent of
language, in these verses, which clearly refer to the
eucharistic practice of the Johannine church. Until this
point in the chapter, up to verse 51b, the symbol of
bread has not been a direct reference to the Eucharist.
Now the symbol is reinterpreted in terms of eating the
flesh and drinking the blood of Jesus. Unlike the Synoptic Gospels, the Fourth Gospel does not contain an
account of the institution of the Eucharist at the Last
Supper. But the statement "the bread that I shall give is
my flesh, for the life of the world" is reminiscent of the
institution formula in its Lukan form: "This is my
body which will be given for you" (Lk 22:19).

The development of this eucharistic interpretation
includes some of the same themes as the preceding discourse: the gift of eternal life, the different eschatological perspectives (verse 54), and the background
of the Exodus story (verse 58). It is almost as though
we have a second version of the bread-of-life discourse,
with the focus not on Jesus' identity but on his sacramental presence.

In fact there are reasons to believe that these verses
—probably we should include verse 59 with them—did
not stand in an earlier version of the Gospel but were
added in order to give prominence to the Eucharist in

the context of the symbol of bread, where it is obviously appropriate. The best reason is the sharp inconsistency between the "flesh" here, which is necessary for eternal life, and the "flesh" in verse 63, which "has nothing to offer." It is very hard to imagine that these two radically different uses of the word could have been intended to stand side by side without some explanation.

The interpretation of the Eucharist found here is very characteristic of the Gospel of John. It gives no hint of the dimension of a community meal but emphasizes the personal relationship of the communicant with Jesus. Just as the living Father is the source of Jesus' life, so the flesh and blood of Jesus are the source of the communicant's life. In the long discourse of Jesus after the Last Supper, the parallel relationships of the Father and Jesus and of Jesus and his believing disciples will be taken up again, but without reference to the Eucharist.

STUDY QUESTION: Compare the understanding of the Eucharist here with the Last Supper account in Luke 22 and with the instructions of Paul in 1 Corinthians 11.

## John 6:59–71
## WHO SHALL WE GO TO?

⁵⁹ He taught this doctrine at Capernaum, in the
⁶⁰ synagogue. ·After hearing it, many of his followers said, "This is intolerable language. How
⁶¹ could anyone accept it?" ·Jesus was aware that
his followers were complaining about it and said,
⁶² "Does this upset you? ·What if you should see
the Son of Man ascend to where he was before?

⁶³ "It is the spirit that gives life,
the flesh has nothing to offer.
The words I have spoken to you are spirit
and they are life.

⁶⁴ "But there are some of you who do not believe." For Jesus knew from the outset those who
did not believe, and who it was that would betray
⁶⁵ him. ·He went on, "This is why I told you that no
one could come to me unless the Father allows
⁶⁶ him." ·After this, many of his disciples left him
and stopped going with him.
⁶⁷ Then Jesus said to the Twelve, "What about
⁶⁸ you, do you want to go away too?" ·Simon Peter
answered, "Lord, who shall we go to? You have
⁶⁹ the message of eternal life, ·and we believe; we
⁷⁰ know that you are the Holy One of God." ·Jesus
replied, "Have I not chosen you, you Twelve?

71 Yet one of you is a devil." ·He meant Judas son
    of Simon Iscariot, since this was the man, one of
    the Twelve, who was going to betray him.

✠

The very different reactions of Jesus' disciples ("followers" in verses 60–61) again depict the range of responses to him that we find elsewhere in the Gospel.
Some complain, or "murmur," (verse 61) at his words;
some (perhaps the same ones) cease being his disciples
altogether. Others, the Twelve, for whom Peter is
spokesman, confess their faith in him as Messiah, the
"Holy One of God." One of them, Judas Iscariot, will
ultimately betray Jesus.

These responses, particularly the rejection of Jesus,
must be understood on three different levels. First, at
an earlier stage of the Gospel when the eucharistic passage was not present, the "intolerable language" to
which many objected was Jesus' statement that he was
the bread that came down from heaven. Verse 60
would follow quite naturally immediately after verse
51a. Moreover, Jesus' remarks in verses 62–64 do not
take up the issue of eating the flesh but rather the issue
of believing in the one who descends from heaven and
will reascend. The issue on this level is Christology.

Secondly, as the text now stands, the "intolerable
language" has become Jesus' statement about the Eucharist. One can readily imagine how even some people
attracted to Jesus would balk at his startling emphasis
on eating his flesh and drinking his blood. The reader
need not, however, try to imagine a historical situation

in which Jesus confronted his followers with such a choice. The Eucharist has been made the issue at this level by the process of composition of the Gospel.

Thirdly, we must remember here as in other places that the Gospel addresses the situation of its own time, near the end of the first century, in the Johannine church. That church is aware of some other Christians who have embraced false ideas and thus ceased to be "disciples" of Jesus. It is not easy to decide whether the issue at this level is the eucharistic practice of the church or its christological faith. Perhaps both are at issue, for if one does not understand that the human Jesus is really the divine Son who has come from the Father, then the Eucharist too has become meaningless.

The final scene with the Twelve reminds us again that the evangelist is reinterpreting the tradition about Jesus. For access to the tradition we may turn to Mark 8:27–33, the story of the confession of messianic faith on the part of Peter at Caesarea Philippi. Jesus' question in Mark, "But you, who do you say I am?" becomes in John "What about you, do you want to go away too?" Peter speaks for the disciples in both cases. In Mark, the confession of faith is followed by the first of Jesus' predictions of the passion; John refers to the betrayal by Judas at the same point. Chapter 8 of Mark gives other indications of a common tradition underlying the two Gospels (in the event John did not know Mark directly): These are a multiplication of the loaves, a demand for a sign, a crossing of the lake, and a discussion about bread.

Peter's statement beautifully concludes the long chapter, for the "message of eternal life" sums up a theme that has dominated the whole discourse. The disciples can rise to such a lofty faith because they have witnessed the manifestation of divine glory in the walking on the water.

STUDY QUESTIONS: How does the Eucharist express Christian faith in who Jesus is? Is being a follower of Jesus a necessary consequence of believing in him?

## John 7:1–30
# HE IS LEADING THE PEOPLE ASTRAY

<sup>1</sup> 7 After this Jesus stayed in Galilee; he could not stay in Judaea, because the Jews were out to kill him.

<sup>2</sup> As the Jewish feast of Tabernacles drew near, <sup>3</sup> his brothers said to him, "Why not leave this place and go to Judaea, and let your disciples see the <sup>4</sup> works you are doing; ·if a man wants to be known he does not do things in secret; since you are doing all this, you should let the whole world see." <sup>5</sup> Not even his brothers, in fact, had faith in him. <sup>6</sup> Jesus answered, "The right time for me has not come yet, but any time is the right time for you. <sup>7</sup> The world cannot hate you, but it does hate me, <sup>8</sup> because I give evidence that its ways are evil. ·Go up to the festival yourselves: I am not going to this festival, because for me the time is not ripe <sup>9</sup> yet." ·Having said that, he stayed behind in Galilee.

<sup>10</sup> However, after his brothers had left for the festival, he went up as well, but quite privately, with- <sup>11</sup> out drawing attention to himself. ·At the festival the Jews were on the lookout for him: "Where is <sup>12</sup> he?" they said. ·People stood in groups whispering about him. Some said, "He is a good man"; others, <sup>13</sup> "No, he is leading the people astray." ·Yet no one spoke about him openly, for fear of the Jews.

¹⁴   When the festival was half over, Jesus went to
¹⁵ the Temple and began to teach. ·The Jews were
astonished and said, "How did he learn to read?
¹⁶ He has not been taught." ·Jesus answered them:

"My teaching is not from myself:
it comes from the one who sent me;
¹⁷   and if anyone is prepared to do his will,
he will know whether my teaching is from God
or whether my doctrine is my own.
¹⁸   When a man's doctrine is his own
he is hoping to get honor for himself;
but when he is working for the honor of one
      who sent him,
then he is sincere
and by no means an impostor.
¹⁹   Did not Moses give you the Law?
And yet not one of you keeps the Law!

²⁰ "Why do you want to kill me?" ·The crowd replied, "You are mad! Who wants to kill you?"
²¹ Jesus answered, "One work I did, and you are all
²² surprised by it. ·Moses ordered you to practice
circumcision—not that it began with him, it goes
back to the patriarchs—and you circumcise on the
²³ sabbath. ·Now if a man can be circumcised on the
sabbath so that the Law of Moses is not broken,
why are you angry with me for making a man
²⁴ whole and complete on a sabbath? ·Do not keep
judging according to appearances; let your judgment be according to what is right."
²⁵   Meanwhile some of the people of Jerusalem
were saying, "Isn't this the man they want to kill?"
²⁶ And here he is, speaking freely, and they have
nothing to say to him! Can it be true the authorities have made up their minds that he is the Christ?
²⁷ Yet we all know where he comes from, but when
the Christ appears no one will know where he
comes from."
²⁸   Then, as Jesus taught in the Temple, he cried
out:

"Yes, you know me and you know where I
    came from.
Yet I have not come of myself:
no, there is one who sent me and I really come
    from him,
and you do not know him,

29    but I know him
because I have come from him
and it was he who sent me."

30    They would have arrested him then, but because his time had not yet come no one laid a
hand on him.

✠

Chapters 7 and 8 contain a series of discourses of
Jesus set in the context of sometimes fierce controversy
between Jesus and "the Jews." The place is the Temple
precincts in Jerusalem, and the time is the early autumn
Feast of Tabernacles. We have divided the discourses
somewhat arbitrarily into four sections for comment.
From a literary point of view, this part of the Gospel
leaves something to be desired. It is repetitious, often
disjointed, and quite lacking in plausible motivations.
But two themes bind it together, and they are central to
the dynamic of the Book of Signs. One is the issue of
Jesus' identity in relationship to the Father, approached
in a variety of ways, and the other is the ever-mounting
tension between Jesus and his adversaries. The Gospel
is a theological statement. We must beware of reading
it on the level of a psychological drama. Were we to do
that, the opposition Jesus meets would sometimes appear self-induced. In a way it is, but we must regard the

provocation theologically as the encounter produced by the revealing word of God in the world.

We have already mentioned the way in which chapter 7 seems to follow closely on chapter 5 (see the commentary on 5:1–18). The plot to kill Jesus in 7:1, 19, 25 recalls 5:18. The sabbath healing mentioned in 7:23 refers to the paralytic of 5:1–18, and this is Jesus' second direct answer (see 5:17) to the charge of sabbath violation in 5:16. If chapters 5 and 6 are not out of order, then we must suppose the evangelist had additional controversy and discourse material left over, as it were, from chapter 5 which he chose to incorporate here.

The opening scene has puzzled many readers. Jesus refuses to go to Jerusalem for the feast and then goes. But we should hesitate to call Jesus indecisive in the Fourth Gospel. He is anything but that. In antiquity, copyists of the Gospel tried to smooth over the paradoxical behavior of Jesus by the insertion of the word "yet" in verse 8: "I am not yet going to this festival." But the modern interpreter has to wrestle with the more problematic text.

Two main points are made in the first eleven verses. First, Jesus refuses to "come out in the open" on any terms but his own. The device of refusing to go and then going is apparently John's way of making this point, for he depicts a very similar situation in the Lazarus story in chapter 11. Secondly, the evangelist uses the opportunity to heighten the theme of the rejection of Jesus by "his own" by showing that even Jesus' relatives did not believe in him (verse 5). Here he picks up a motif from the tradition about Jesus, attested in Mark 6:4 and elsewhere, that Jesus' relatives were slow to come to faith in him. The tradition is not implausible and is hardly likely to have been invented by the early Christians, especially in view of the prominence of some of Jesus' "brothers," such as James, in the early church. This note of unbelief is an appropriate introduction to the conflicts in the ensuing chapters.

When Jesus arrives in Jerusalem, the other main theme is introduced in the speculation about Jesus' own person (verse 12). "Leading the people astray" was probably a legal offense in Judaism. In any case the charge of being a "deceiver" was part of the Jewish polemic against Jesus and it is reflected in Matthew 27:63 (where the JB translates "impostor"). Two questions are raised about Jesus: Where did he get his learning? And how can he be the Messiah if people know where he comes from? Jesus transforms both issues into statements about his relationship to the Father, and it is this which dominates the remainder of the section for the most part.

STUDY QUESTIONS: How does one distinguish between a genuinely inquiring faith and mere religious curiosity? Does this passage reflect the difference?

## John 7:31–52
# HE WAS SPEAKING OF THE SPIRIT

<sup>31</sup> There were many people in the crowds, however, who believed in him; they were saying, "When the Christ comes, will he give more signs <sup>32</sup> than this man?" ·Hearing that rumors like this about him were spreading among the people, the Pharisees sent the Temple police to arrest him.

<sup>33</sup> Then Jesus said:

"I shall remain with you for only a short time now;
then I shall go back to the one who sent me.
<sup>34</sup> You will look for me and will not find me:
where I am
you cannot come."

<sup>35</sup> The Jews then said to one another, "Where is he going that we shan't be able to find him? Is he going abroad to the people who are dispersed among the Greeks and will he teach the Greeks? <sup>36</sup> What does he mean when he says:

'You will look for me and will not find me:
where I am,
you cannot come?' "

<sup>37</sup> On the last day and greatest day of the festival, Jesus stood there and cried out:

"If any man is thirsty, let him come to me!
38      Let the man come and drink ·who believes in
me!"

As scripture says: From his breast shall flow
fountains of living water.
39      He was speaking of the Spirit which those who
believed in him were to receive; for there was no
Spirit as yet because Jesus had not yet been glorified.
40      Several people who had been listening said,
41  "Surely he must be the prophet," ·and some said,
"He is the Christ," but others said, "Would the
42  Christ be from Galilee? ·Does not scripture say
that the Christ must be descended from David
43  and come from the town of Bethlehem?" ·So the
44  people could not agree about him. ·Some would
have liked to arrest him, but no one actually laid
hands on him.
45      The police went back to the chief priests and
Pharisees who said to them, "Why haven't you
46  brought him?" ·The police replied, "There has
never been anybody who has spoken like him."
47  "So," the Pharisees answered, "you have been led
48  astray as well? ·Have any of the authorities be-
49  lieved in him? Any of the Pharisees? ·This rabble
knows nothing about the Law—they are damned."
50  One of them, Nicodemus—the same man who had
51  come to Jesus earlier—said to them, ·"But surely
the Law does not allow us to pass judgment on a
man without giving him a hearing and discover-
52  ing what he is about?" ·To this they answered,
"Are you a Galilean too? Go into the matter,
and see for yourself: prophets do not come out
of Galilee."

☩

As the conflict continues, there are still some who
are attracted to faith in Jesus as Messiah (verse 31),

but it is a faith based merely on signs and it will not prove durable. Nicodemus, who represented such a faith in 3:2, reappears as the spokesman for a very fair and reasonable position. But there is no indication that he has gone beyond his initial signs-faith.

One of the many examples of Johannine irony in this section is to be found in verse 35. The reaction of the Jews is literalistic: If Jesus is going where we cannot come, can he be going abroad to mingle with gentiles? The irony is perceptible only to the reader who knows that when this Gospel was written, the Christian mission had brought the message of Jesus to the Jews dispersed among the gentiles and that the churches were in most cases largely made up of gentiles.

Verses 37–39 have long occasioned problems for the reader of the Fourth Gospel, but these ought not to obscure the richness of the imagery which John himself interprets for us. As read by the JB, the quotation in verse 38 apparently refers to Jesus, and this is in harmony with the Christocentrism of the whole Gospel. When Jesus has been glorified in the passion-resurrection, he will in fact confer the Spirit on his disciples (20:22). This reading seems preferable, but there is another option, and many have taken it. Punctuation is missing from the oldest manuscripts; by adopting a different punctuation, one can translate: "If anyone is thirsty let him come to me and drink. Whoever believes in me, as scripture says, from his breast shall flow fountains of living water." The idea that the believer in turn becomes a source of living water is not foreign to John (see 4:14). The reader should, here as elsewhere, be aware of the options and decide which better fits a total understanding of the Gospel.

As for the "scripture" quoted in verse 38, though it sounds a little like several Old Testament passages dealing with the theme of wisdom (e.g., Pr 18:4), it is not a direct citation from any passage we can identify.

The chapter ends with speculation about the identity of Jesus—which occurs often in John—on the part of the crowd first and then on the part of the Jewish leaders. They cannot agree whether Jesus is the prophet like Moses or the Messiah, or perhaps both at once. As we have seen before and will see again in chapter 8, all such speculation misses the mark. The true identity of Jesus cannot be grasped adequately by categorizing him, even in biblical categories. It can only be seen on his own terms: Jesus is the Son in whom the Father is revealed.

A very old manuscript of John, discovered not long ago, has a reading which makes the end of verse 52 agree with verse 40 and which gets rid of the awkward statement that no prophet comes from Galilee: It inserts an article and reads, "The prophet does not come out of Galilee." Older manuscripts are not always better ones, however, and it may be that this one was smoothing out the difficulties here.

STUDY QUESTION: How do the gift of the Spirit, the revelation of the Father, and eternal life relate to one another in the Fourth Gospel?

## John 7:53 to 8:11
## NEITHER DO I CONDEMN YOU

<sup>53</sup><sup>1</sup> They all went home, **8** and Jesus went to the Mount of Olives.

**2** At daybreak he appeared in the Temple again; and as all the people came to him, he sat down and began to teach them.

**3** The scribes and Pharisees brought a woman along who had been caught committing adultery; and making her stand there in full view of every-

**4** body, ·they said to Jesus, "Master, this woman was caught in the very act of committing adultery,

**5** and Moses has ordered us in the Law to condemn women like this to death by stoning. What have

**6** you to say?" ·They asked him this as a test, looking for something to use against him. But Jesus bent down and started writing on the ground with

**7** his finger. ·As they persisted with their question, he looked up and said, "If there is one of you who has not sinned, let him be the first to throw

**8** a stone at her." ·Then he bent down and wrote

**9** on the ground again. ·When they heard this they went away one by one, beginning with the eldest, until Jesus was left alone with the woman, who

**10** remained standing there. ·He looked up and said, "Woman, where are they? Has no one con-

¹¹ demned you?" ·"No one, sir," she replied. "Neither do I condemn you," said Jesus, "go away and
don't sin any more."

✠

As was pointed out in the Introduction, this story is
certainly not an original part of the Fourth Gospel.
Nevertheless it is a magnificent story and has rightly
been for centuries a prized glimpse of Jesus exercising a
wisdom akin to Solomon's and a compassion without
parallel. The tone of the story reminds us of Luke, but
it probably does not come directly from the synoptic
tradition. Many think it originated in some ancient gospel, not one of the four in our New Testament, that has
not survived. Eventually the story outlived its source
and became attached to the Fourth Gospel in some
branches of the manuscript tradition. It is hard to say
why it was added here, but the introduction to it fits
more or less plausibly and the theme of judgment in it
is mentioned in 8:15–16.

It is not immediately clear why the question of the
scribes and Pharisees constituted a "test" or trap for
Jesus. We have to suppose something like the following. The Jewish court has legally convicted the woman
and sentenced her to death according to the Mosaic
Law (see Lv 20:10). But the Roman authorities in
Palestine do not permit the Jews to exercise capital
punishment. If Jesus advises against execution, he is in
conflict with the Law. If he recommends it, he is in
trouble with the Romans.

Jesus skillfully evades the trap by refusing to answer

the question. People have speculated endlessly about what Jesus was writing on the ground, as though that would contain a clue to the story. But they may be missing the point. His action is a diversion of attention, meaning simply that he refuses to accept the dilemma thrust upon him, and in fact the trap vanishes as the scribes and Pharisees walk away. It is important to note that Jesus does not condone adultery in this story, nor does he comment on the Mosaic Law. What he does is show mercy.

STUDY QUESTIONS: What is distinctive in the behavior of Jesus in this story? How can the modern Christian formulate a position with respect to law, justice, and mercy?

## John 8:12–30
# I AM THE LIGHT OF THE WORLD

12    When Jesus spoke to the people again, he said:

> "I am the light of the world;
> anyone who follows me will not be walking in the dark;
> he will have the light of life."

13    At this the Pharisees said to him, "You are testifying on your own behalf; your testimony is not
14 valid." ·Jesus replied:

> "It is true that I am testifying on my own behalf,
> but my testimony is still valid,
> because I know
> where I came from and where I am going;
> but you do not know
> where I come from or where I am going.
15 You judge by human standards;
> I judge no one,
16 but if I judge,
> my judgment will be sound,
> because I am not alone:
> the one who sent me is with me;
17 and in your Law it is written
> that the testimony of two witnesses is valid.

18    I may be testifying on my own behalf,
       but the Father who sent me is my witness too."

19    They asked him, "Where is your Father?" Jesus answered:

      "You do not know me, nor do you know my Father;
      if you did know me, you would know my Father as well."

20    He spoke these words in the Treasury, while teaching in the Temple. No one arrested him, because his time had not yet come.

21    Again he said to them:

      "I am going away; you will look for me
      and you will die in your sin.
      Where I am going, you cannot come."

22    The Jews said to one another, "Will he kill himself? Is that what he means by saying, 'Where I
23  am going, you cannot come?'" ·Jesus went on:

      "You are from below;
      I am from above.
      You are of this world;
      I am not of this world.
24    I have told you already: You will die in your sins.
      Yes, if you do not believe that I am He,
      you will die in your sins."

25    So they said to him, "Who are you?" Jesus answered:

      "What I have told you from the outset.
26    About you I have much to say
      and much to condemn;
      but the one who sent me is truthful,
      and what I have learned from him
      I declare to the world."

27    They failed to understand that he was talking

<sup>28</sup> to them about the Father. ·So Jesus said:

> "When you have lifted up the Son of Man,
> then you will know that I am He
> and that I do nothing of myself:
> what the Father has taught me
> is what I preach;

<sup>29</sup> he who sent me is with me,
> and has not left me to myself,
> for I always do what pleases him."

<sup>30</sup> As he was saying this, many came to believe in him.

✠

Chapter 8 continues both the themes and the setting of chapter 7; to appreciate the continuity, the reader should reread chapter 7, skip the story of the adulterous woman, and go on to read chapter 8. One of the ceremonies that characterized the Feast of Tabernacles in the Jerusalem Temple was the lavish illumination of the outer courtyard. It is perhaps with this in mind that the evangelist introduces a new set of discourses of Jesus with the saying "I am the light of the world." The contrast between "walking in the dark" and having "the light of life" is a good introduction to the sharply drawn contrast between "the Jews" and Jesus that permeates the whole chapter. But the Gospel does not draw out the full implications of Jesus as the light of the world until chapter 9 (see 9:5).

The theme that dominates the whole chapter, with mounting sharpness, is that of fatherhood and sonship. Jesus reveals that God is his Father, beginning with verse 18, and the remaining discourses continue the revelation, which will reach its climax only in chapter 10. In the next section, we will see how the contrast is drawn with the father of Jesus' adversaries.

The first set of discourses and conflict dialogues, verses 13-20, take up again a theme already developed extensively in the discourse of chapter 5, that of witness to Jesus. To understand the contents of the discourses in John, it would help to reread 5:30-47. The evangelist deals with themes somewhat the way a composer deals with thematic elements. He can return to them over and over again, most of the time with variations, occasionally with repetition, and he is not put off by what seem on the surface contradictions. It is the themes that are important. Jesus bears witness to himself (8:18) but also denies it (5:31). With the judgment theme, which we have seen repeatedly in other contexts, Jesus both judges and does not judge (8:15-16; see also, e.g., 3:17 and 5:22). Perhaps in this latter case there are nuances in the word "judge": Jesus does not *condemn* the world but he does exercise judgment by challenging people to respond to his revealing word with a yes of faith or a no of unbelief (or "sin" in John's sense of the term; see 8:21, 24).

The second part of this collection of discourses, verses 21-30, begins and ends with allusions to Jesus' death, contrasted with dying in sin. The language is indirect: Jesus is "going away" (verse 21) and as Son of Man he will be "lifted up" (verse 28). The death of Jesus, as we shall see, is his return to the Father, the completion and the climax of his mission as revealer. At his death his true identity will be known; he is the one who can appropriate for himself the divine name "I am." The use of this expression without (in Greek) any predicate occurs in 8:24, 28, and 58, and in all cases, though one could make sense of the passages otherwise, the allusion to the name of God is most probable.

The episode ends with the statement that "many came to believe in him." As we shall see immediately, however, such belief is shallow and does not last long. To appreciate the Fourth Gospel we have to sort out the types of responses to Jesus for which the evangelist can use the word "believe." Ultimately true faith is belief in Jesus as the one who comes from, reveals in himself, and returns to the Father. The whole Gospel is meant to communicate that.

STUDY QUESTION:    The Fourth Gospel (at least in its
                   Greek original) never uses the noun
                   "faith" but only the verb "to be-
                   lieve" or "to have faith." Can you
                   see a reason for this in Johannine
                   theology?

## John 8:31–59
# THE TRUTH WILL MAKE YOU FREE

<sup>31</sup> To the Jews who believed in him Jesus said:

> "If you make my word your home
> you will indeed be my disciples,
<sup>32</sup>> you will learn the truth
> and the truth shall make you free."

<sup>33</sup> They answered, "We are descended from Abraham and we have never been the slaves of anyone, what do you mean, 'You will be made free?'"
<sup>34</sup> Jesus replied:

> "I tell you most solemnly,
> everyone who commits sin is a slave.
<sup>35</sup>> Now the slave's place in the house is not assured,
> but the son's place is assured.
<sup>36</sup>> So if the Son makes you free,
> you will be free indeed.
<sup>37</sup>> I know that you are descended from Abraham;
> but in spite of that you want to kill me
> because nothing I say has penetrated into you.
<sup>38</sup>> What I, for my part, speak of
> is what I have seen with my Father;
> but you, you put into action
> the lessons learned from your father."

39    They repeated, "Our father is Abraham." Jesus
      said to them:

      "If you were Abraham's children,
      you would do as Abraham did.
40    As it is, you want to kill me
      when I tell you the truth
      as I have learned it from God;
      that is not what Abraham did.
41    What you are doing is what your father does."

      "We were not born of prostitution," they went
42    on, "we have one father: God." ·Jesus answered:

      "If God were your father, you would love me,
      since I have come here from God; yes, I have
          come from him;
      not that I came because I chose,
      no, I was sent, and by him.
43    Do you know why you cannot take in what I
          say?
      It is because you are unable to understand my
          language.
44    The devil is your father,
      and you prefer to do
      what your father wants.
      He was a murderer from the start;
      he was never grounded in the truth;
      there is no truth in him at all:
      when he lies
      he is drawing on his own store,
      because he is a liar, and the father of lies.
45    But as for me, I speak the truth
      and for that very reason,
      you do not believe me.
46    Can one of you convict me of sin?
      If I speak the truth, why do you not believe me?
47    A child of God
      listens to the words of God;
      if you refuse to listen,
      it is because you are not God's children."

⁴⁸ The Jews replied, "Are we not right in saying that you are a Samaritan and possessed by a devil?" Jesus answered:

⁴⁹ "I am not possessed;
no, I honor my Father,
but you want to dishonor me.
⁵⁰ Not that I care for my own glory,
there is someone who takes care of that and is the judge of it.
⁵¹ I tell you most solemnly,
whoever keeps my word
will never see death."

⁵² The Jews said, "Now we know for certain that you are possessed. Abraham is dead, and the prophets are dead, and yet you say, 'Whoever keeps my word will never know the taste of ⁵³ death.' ·Are you greater than our father Abraham, who is dead? The prophets are dead too. ⁵⁴ Who are you claiming to be?" ·Jesus answered:

"If I were to seek my own glory
that would be no glory at all;
my glory is conferred by the Father,
by the one of whom you say, 'He is our God,'
⁵⁵ although you do not know him.
But I know him,
and if I were to say: I do not know him,
I should be a liar, as you are liars yourselves.
But I do know him, and I faithfully keep his word.
⁵⁶ Your father Abraham rejoiced
to think that he would see my Day;
he saw it and was glad."

⁵⁷ The Jews then said, "You are not fifty yet, and ⁵⁸ you have seen Abraham!" ·Jesus replied:

"I tell you most solemnly,
before Abraham ever was,
I Am."

[59]     At this they picked up stones to throw at him;
but Jesus hid himself and left the Temple.

☩

The tension that has been growing throughout chapters 5, 7, and 8 now reaches a climax in the vehemence
of the argument and in the attempt to kill Jesus. It is a
dynamic in which Jesus' revealing word about the Father and his own relationship to him confronts "the
Jews" with the real challenge of faith (verse 31). And
they fail the test. The use of "word" runs like a thread
throughout this section, though the JB translation
sometimes obscures it. It occurs in verses 31, 37
("nothing I say"), 43 ("what I say"), 51, 52, and 55.
In all cases but the last it is Jesus' word which must be
kept, which must be clung to and heard, and which in
return will bring the gift of eternal life. Though it is not
stated explicitly, the implication of Jesus' whole relationship to the Father is that his revealing word is really God's word which he faithfully keeps (verse 55).

That is why the word can be identified with the
truth, and the truth can liberate the slave—one who is
in a state of unbelief, of sin—and make him a free child
of God (see 1:12). Why should the Jews object to this
magisterial promise? They immediately resent the implication that they have been slaves and invoke their
descent from the patriarch Abraham. And as the discourse continues, their hostility grows and becomes im-
penetrable. We have already seen, in the story of the
Samaritan woman at the well, that when Jesus' revealing word confronts a person, it must become a personal

challenge, it must force the person to examine himself or herself and in the light of that make a response. That is what the Jews refuse to do here. Failure to recognize one's unbelief makes coming to faith impossible.

As the conflict unfolds, the issue of who is whose father dominates. The adversaries appeal to Abraham and then to God as their father. And in the sharpest polemical language yet, Jesus calls the devil their father. In Johannine thought as developed here and elsewhere, the lines are very sharply drawn. The only possible answers to the word are yes or no. To reject it is to reject truth, to be in sin, to be a child of the father of lies. To accept it is to learn the truth, to become free, to be a child of God.

The real issue here and throughout the Gospel is the christological one, and so the theme of God as Jesus' Father is developed here in contrast to the claims of the adversaries. Jesus speaks the Father's word, comes from the Father, is sent by him, receives his glory from him. In fact he is the pre-existent divine Son who can rightfully invoke the name "I am."

Sometimes the reader of passages like these may be tempted to feel that it is all somehow unfair. "The Jews" in the Gospel don't seem to have a chance, because Jesus neither reasons with them nor tries to persuade them. Instead he confronts them with symbols, with ambiguity, with challenges. We need to recall three things in response to this. First, the evangelist wrote a theological work in the form of a gospel. He was more interested in issues than in personalities, and, apart from a few passages, he had no concern to portray plausible psychological motivations and reactions. He took the gospel genre seriously, to be sure, but the gospel is always proclamation, not merely narrative.

Secondly, the Fourth Gospel was written with a view to its own time and an awareness of what had in fact happened since the time of Jesus. The Jews known to the evangelist had in fact mostly refused to accept Jesus as the Messiah and Son of God, and their rejection was a factual presupposition of the gospel story. It needed to be recorded, not explained away. And thirdly, there is in the revealing word itself an element of alienness that can only be expressed with a certain ambiguity. It is God speaking in the world of humanity, in human terms of course, but stretching the human beyond itself to an eternal dimension. For this purpose—as to a certain extent in all theological and religious discourse— only symbolic language will do. More important than instant understanding is the willingness to be open to a word from outside ordinary human experience that ultimately reveals latent dimensions of human experience itself. It is a Word made flesh, but at the same time a Word that is with God.

STUDY QUESTION: How does the revealing word of God confront the modern Christian, and how can one be really open to assent to it?

# John 9:1–41
## NOW I CAN SEE

<sup>1</sup> <sup>2</sup> **9** As he went along, he saw a man who had been blind from birth. ·His disciples asked him, "Rabbi, who sinned, this man or his parents, for <sup>3</sup> him to have been born blind?" ·"Neither he nor his parents sinned," Jesus answered, "he was born blind so that the works of God might be displayed in him.

<sup>4</sup>   "As long as the day lasts
     I must carry out the work of the one who sent
        me;
     the night will soon be here when no one can
        work.
<sup>5</sup>   As long as I am in the world
     I am the light of the world."

<sup>6</sup>   Having said this, he spat on the ground, made a paste with the spittle, put this over the eyes of the <sup>7</sup> blind man, ·and said to him, "Go and wash in the Pool of Siloam (a name that means "sent"). So the blind man went off and washed himself, and came away with his sight restored.
<sup>8</sup>   His neighbors and people who earlier had seen him begging said, "Isn't this the man who used to <sup>9</sup> sit and beg?" ·Some said, "Yes, it is the same one." Others said, "No, he only looks like him."

10 The man himself said, "I am the man." ·So they
said to him, "Then how do your eyes come to be
11 open?" ·"The man called Jesus" he answered,
"made a paste, daubed my eyes with it and said
to me, 'Go and wash at Siloam'; so I went, and
12 when I washed I could see." ·They asked, "Where
is he?" "I don't know," he answered.

13    They brought the man who had been blind to
14 the Pharisees. ·It had been a sabbath day when
Jesus made the paste and opened the man's eyes,
15 so when the Pharisees asked him how he had come
to see, he said, "He put a paste on my eyes, and I
16 washed, and I can see." ·Then some of the Pharisees said, "This man cannot be from God: he
does not keep the sabbath." Others said, "How
could a sinner produce signs like this?" And there
17 was disagreement among them. ·So they spoke to
the blind man again, "What have you to say about
him yourself, now that he has opened your eyes?"
"He is a prophet," replied the man.

18    However, the Jews would not believe that the
man had been blind and had gained his sight,
19 without first sending for his parents and ·asking
them, "Is this man really your son who you say
was born blind? If so, how is it that he is now able
20 to see?" ·His parents answered, "We know he is
21 our son and we know he was born blind, ·but we
don't know how it is that he can see now, or who
opened his eyes. He is old enough: let him speak
22 for himself." ·His parents spoke like this out of
fear of the Jews, who had already agreed to expel
from the synagogue anyone who should acknowl-
23 edge Jesus as the Christ. ·This was why his parents
said, "He is old enough; ask him."

24    So the Jews again sent for the man and said to
him, "Give glory to God! For our part, we know
25 that this man is a sinner." ·The man answered,
"I don't know if he is a sinner; I only know that I
26 was blind and now I can see." ·They said to him,
"What did he do to you? How did he open your

27 eyes?" ·He replied, "I have told you once and you
wouldn't listen. Why do you want to hear it all
again? Do you want to become his disciples too?"

28 At this they hurled abuse at him: "You can be his
disciple," they said, "we are disciples of Moses:

29 we know that God spoke to Moses, but as for this

30 man, we don't know where he comes from." ·The
man replied, "Now here is an astonishing thing!
He has opened my eyes, and you don't know

31 where he comes from! ·We know that God doesn't
listen to sinners, but God does listen to men who

32 are devout and do his will. ·Ever since the world
began it is unheard of for anyone to open the eyes

33 of a man who was born blind; ·if this man were not

34 from God, he couldn't do a thing." ·"Are you try-
ing to teach us," they replied, "and you a sinner
through and through, since you were born!" And
they drove him away.

35      Jesus heard they had driven him away, and
when he found him he said to him, "Do you be-

36 lieve in the Son of Man?" ·"Sir," the man replied,
"tell me who he is so that I may believe in him."

37 Jesus said, "You are looking at him; he is speak-

38 ing to you." ·The man said, "Lord, I believe," and
worshiped him.

39      Jesus said:

"It is for judgment
that I have come into this world,
so that those without sight may see
and those with sight turn blind."

40 Hearing this, some Pharisees who were present

41 said to him, "We are not blind, surely?" ·Jesus replied:

"Blind? If you were,
you would not be guilty,
but since you say, 'We see,'
your guilt remains.

✠

The literary character of the Gospel changes radically with the introduction of another miracle story. But though all the classic elements of a miracle story are present, it is obvious that this episode is much more than that. Several healings of blind men are to be found in the synoptic tradition, and it is not possible to say which particular story is being reinterpreted here.

The story is a long one, but it is so carefully constructed that one cannot divide it up for the purposes of commentary. The underlying literary principle is derived from classical drama: it is the so-called law of stage duality, by which a scene is identified as two characters or groups of characters in dialogue on the stage. If we analyze the chapter according to this principle, we find a drama in seven scenes, symmetrically arranged, roughly as the JB translation divides the paragraphs, as follows:

| | | |
|---|---|---|
| A  | 1–7   | Jesus and the disciples |
| B  | 8–12  | The blind man and his neighbors |
| C  | 13–17 | The blind man and the Pharisees |
| D  | 18–23 | The Pharisees and the parents |
| C′ | 24–34 | The blind man and the Pharisees |
| B′ | 35–38 | The blind man and Jesus |
| A′ | 39–41 | Jesus and the Pharisees |

What is the drama about? If the question seems hard to answer, it is only because there are so many plot lines to follow up. Let us try to list some of them. First, Jesus performs another sign (verse 16), which characteristically elicits various reactions from those who behold it, ranging from faith on the part of the formerly blind man to rejection on the part of the Pharisees. The sign of giving sight (light) to a man born blind (in perpetual darkness) illustrates in action Jesus' saying "I am the light of the world." We should probably prefer a different reading of verse 4 than the one the JB has chosen: many ancient texts read "*We* must carry out the work of the one who sent me." This seemingly incongruous mixture of pronouns may be quite deliberate. It implies that Jesus is inviting the disciples to join him in the work of the Father (see 4:31–38), which of course is not really performing miracles but bringing people to faith, giving "sight" to the spiritually blind.

Secondly, there is the issue of sin, which is introduced as a red-herring issue by the disciples in the first scene (verse 2), calling upon the ancient biblical tradition that the sins of the fathers are visited upon the children (see Ex 20:5). The issue returns in the last scene—it is the Greek word for sin that is translated "guilty" and "guilt" in the JB in verse 41—where "sin" is understood in the Johannine sense of unbelief. The Pharisees' reaction to the sign is to solidify their sinful refusal to believe in Jesus. Note also how the issue of sin is ironically raised about both Jesus (verse 24) and the man born blind (verse 34).

Thirdly, there is the issue of christological titles, which progress from prophet in verse 17, to Messiah (Christ) in verse 22, to Son of Man in verse 35. Only the last serves as a basis for real faith on the part of the blind man, because it is Jesus himself who uses it. The formal and almost liturgical response of the man in verse 38 is uncharacteristic of the Fourth Gospel and is probably to be regarded as a later addition arising from the baptismal practice of the church.

Fourthly, there is the personal drama of the man born blind. Like the Samaritan woman at the well, he stands out in the Gospel as a real personality, even though he remains nameless. His stubborn defense of the "facts" of his cure leads him along the road to faith in Jesus, though he pays a heavy penalty of ostracism for it. Few subordinate characters in this Gospel emerge with any personal delineation, but this man is surely one of them. In the end he is a model of the Christian believer who suffers for his faith. And the evangelist allows him some intriguingly ironic lines in the play (e.g., verse 27).

Finally, there is the second level of meaning in the drama, which refers not to the time of Jesus but to the events in the Johannine church subsequent to the time of Jesus. The clue here lies in the symmetrical arrangement of scenes which gives prominence to the central scene in which the Pharisees confront the parents of the man born blind. (We will observe a similar structural technique in the Johannine passion narrative.) On the surface, this scene seems to add little to the story, but in reality its prominence must be taken seriously. The parents, who are of course Jews, react out of fear of "the Jews"—already this strange language alerts the reader to the special meaning of "the Jews" for John. The language of verse 22 is highly technical: "the Jews" have formally determined that if anyone acknowledges that Jesus is the Messiah, that person is to be expelled from the synagogue (see also 12:42 and 16:2). It was only very late in the first century A.D. that the Jews had taken such a formal action, and we must infer from this Gospel that such an expulsion had been the fate of the Johannine community. The process is dramatized here in the experience of the man born blind, who in verse 34 is actually expelled. The very poignancy of this expulsion from their Jewish heritage and roots helps to explain the severely negative reaction of the Gospel of John to "the Jews."

Like any good story, this is a rich one precisely because it has multiple story lines and even multiple levels of significance. It deserves to be read and reread with an eye to typical Johannine themes and language.

STUDY QUESTIONS: For the modern Christian, what are the consequences of faith in Jesus? Is some sort of social ostracism an inevitable consequence? If so, why?

# John 10:1–21
## I AM THE GOOD SHEPHERD

¹ **10** "I tell you most solemnly, anyone who does not enter the sheepfold through the gate, but gets in some other way is a thief and a brig- ² and. ·The one who enters through the gate is the ³ shepherd of the flock; ·the gatekeeper lets him in, the sheep hear his voice, one by one he calls his ⁴ own sheep and leads them out. ·When he has brought out his flock, he goes ahead of them, and the sheep follow because they know his voice. ⁵ They never follow a stranger but run away from him: they do not recognize the voice of stran- gers."

⁶ Jesus told them this parable but they failed to understand what he meant by telling it to them.

⁷ So Jesus spoke to them again:

"I tell you most solemnly,
I am the gate of the sheepfold.
⁸ All others who have come
are thieves and brigands;
but the sheep took no notice of them.
⁹ I am the gate.
Anyone who enters through me will be safe:
he will go freely in and out
and be sure of finding pasture.
¹⁰ The thief comes
only to steal and kill and destroy.

I have come
so that they may have life
and have it to the full.

11  I am the good shepherd:
the good shepherd is one who lays down his life
for his sheep.

12  The hired man, since he is not the shepherd
and the sheep do not belong to him,
abandons the sheep and runs away
as soon as he sees a wolf coming,
and then the wolf attacks and scatters the
sheep;

13  this is because he is only a hired man
and has no concern for the sheep.

14  I am the good shepherd;
I know my own
and my own know me,

15  just as the Father knows me
and I know the Father;
and I lay down my life for my sheep.

16  And there are other sheep I have
that are not of this fold,
and these I have to lead as well.
They too will listen to my voice,
and there will be only one flock,
and one shepherd.

17  The Father loves me,
because I lay down my life
in order to take it up again.

18  No one takes it from me;
I lay it down of my own free will,
and as it is in my power to lay it down,
so it is in my power to take it up again;
and this is the command I have been given by
my Father."

19  These words caused disagreement among the
20  Jews. ·Many said, "He is possessed, he is raving;
21  why bother to listen to him?" ·Others said, "These
are not the words of a man possessed by a devil:
could a devil open the eyes of the blind?"

✠

One of the most striking differences between the Jesus of the Synoptic Gospels and the Jesus of the Fourth Gospel is the almost complete absence of parables in the latter. The use of parables is one of the most characteristic features of Jesus' preaching in the Synoptics, and scholars are in broad agreement that parables were historically a mark of Jesus' authentic utterances. This passage in John is the only one where anything like parables are recorded, but even though the image of the gate is called a "parable" in verse 6, the word used in Greek is not the ordinary word for parable in the Synoptics.

Whatever they should be called, we have here some carefully developed figures of speech which center around two more "I am" sayings with predicates: "I am the gate" and "I am the good shepherd." The two images are quite separate and are used to make quite different points. The first issue, connected with the gate image, is one of access: How does one find access to God, or to life? Through Jesus. The second issue is a christological one which focuses even more directly on the person of Jesus. Jesus is the model shepherd, who in fact lays down his life, in the passion sequence, for the benefit of his flock, both those who believe in him as members of the Johannine community and the "other sheep," who are probably members of other Christian churches.

The background of the shepherd-sheep imagery is of course extensive in the Bible, and though it may require some interpretation for modern Western, urban society, it was of universal significance for the biblical authors. The Old Testament background here may be the familiar language of Psalm 23, "Yahweh is my shepherd," where the evangelist would not hesitate to attribute a divine epithet to Jesus. Or it may be the prophecy of Ezekiel (34:1–31) regarding the shepherds of Israel, whose infidelity is contrasted with Yahweh as his own shepherd and his servant David, whom he will raise up as a model of what a responsible shepherd should be. In the gospel tradition of the New Testament, which the fourth evangelist is doubtless reinterpreting here, one thinks of the parable of the lost sheep in Luke 15:4–7 and Matthew 18:12–14.

In contrast to the rest of chapter 10, this section has no explicit setting, but it clearly follows on the healing of the blind man in chapter 9, which is referred to in 10:21. Since it concerns the responsibility of religious leaders—and of course the role of Jesus himself—it may well be understood as addressed to the "blind" Pharisees of the preceding episode.

STUDY QUESTION: What are the implications of Jesus' shepherd parables for contemporary religious leadership?

## John 10:22–42
# THE FATHER AND I ARE ONE

22  It was the time when the feast of Dedication
was being celebrated in Jerusalem. It was winter,
23  and Jesus was in the Temple walking up and down
24  in the Portico of Solomon. ·The Jews gathered
around him and said, "How much longer are you
going to keep us in suspense? If you are the Christ,
25  tell us plainly." ·Jesus replied:

"I have told you, but you do not believe.
The works I do in my Father's name are my
    witness;
26  but you do not believe,
because you are no sheep of mine.
27  The sheep that belong to me listen to my voice;
I know them and they follow me.
28  I give them eternal life;
they will never be lost
and no one will ever steal them from me.
29  The Father who gave them to me is greater
    than anyone,
and no one can steal from the Father.
30  The Father and I are one."

31  The Jews fetched stones to stone him, ·so Jesus
32  said to them, "I have done many good works
for you to see, works from my Father; for which

³³ of these are you stoning me?" ·The Jews answered him, "We are not stoning you for doing a
good work but for blasphemy: you are only a man
³⁴ and you claim to be God." ·Jesus answered:

"Is it not written in your Law:
I said, you are gods?
³⁵ So the Law uses the word gods
of those to whom the word of God was addressed,
and scripture cannot be rejected.
³⁶ Yet you say to someone the Father has conse-
crated and sent into the world,
'You are blaspheming,'
because he says, 'I am the Son of God.'
³⁷ If I am not doing my Father's work,
there is no need to believe me;
³⁸ but if I am doing it,
then even if you refuse to believe in me,
at least believe in the work I do;
then you will know for sure
that the Father is in me and I am in the Father."

³⁹ They wanted to arrest him then, but he eluded
them.
⁴⁰ He went back again to the far side of the Jordan
to stay in the district where John had once been
⁴¹ baptizing. ·Many people who came to him there
said, "John gave no signs, but all he said about this
⁴² man was true"; ·and many of them believed in
him.

✠

This last encounter between Jesus and "the Jews"
has an air of finality about it and brings to a climax the
issue of the identity of Jesus. The evangelist places it

on another occasion, the December Feast of Dedication
or Hanukkah, but nothing in the discourses has any
particular reference to that occasion. In fact, the use of
the metaphor of sheep (verses 26–28) connects this
passage with the previous one. Several details in the
passage remind us of the trial of Jesus before the Jews
in the Markan passion tradition (see Mk 14:53–65):
for example, the request "If you are the Christ, tell us
plainly" (verse 24), and the charge of blasphemy
(verse 33). It is quite possible that John had in mind
the trial scene. It is certain that he oriented this passage
toward the passion, for it sets up a reason for the arrest
and final conviction of Jesus. The next chapter will introduce quite a different reason, the success of Jesus as
a result of the raising of Lazarus, but perhaps placing
these two motivations side by side is an indication that
there was discussion about the issue in the Johannine
church.

The main focus is again on who Jesus is, and now,
much more explicitly than before, Jesus speaks out.
Three statements should be noted in particular. In
verse 25 Jesus clearly if indirectly claims to be the
Messiah (Christ): "I have told you." Then in verse 30
he claims a certain identity with the Father which his
adversaries clearly understand to be a claim to divinity.
We must be careful not to press this verse too closely,
however, as Christians of later centuries did in the controversies about the Trinity. It does not speak either of
one person or of one nature. Finally in verse 36 Jesus
speaks of himself as the one who says, "I am the Son of
God." Throughout the passage Jesus appeals to his
doing the works of the Father as evidence to support
these claims. Here especially we must give full value to
the expression "works": They are the signs, to be sure,

but they are also the revealing word of Jesus, both of which are intended to bring about faith.

In verse 34 Jesus quotes Psalm 82:6, attributing it to "your Law" as a general name for the whole Old Testament. The argument is a peculiar one, at least to a modern reader. It seems to say that if scripture, which is God's word, can call human beings "gods," then a fortiori it is not blasphemy for Jesus to call himself God's Son. It may be that this kind of argument reflects scriptural debates between Jews and Christians of a later time.

John the Baptist is mentioned for the last time at the end of this chapter, and again it is the quality of his witness to Jesus that is singled out. Even though John did not display the credentials of a prophet, that is, he gave no signs, his testimony to Jesus has proved to be true. We are not told, however, how this happened for the people across the Jordan, but as readers of the Gospel we understand.

STUDY QUESTION: The issue of Jesus' relationship to the Father has come to a conclusion for the Book of Signs. Sum up all the things said about it so far. This will prepare for what the discourse after the Supper has to add to the picture.

## John 11:1–44
# LET US GO TOO, AND DIE WITH HIM

¹ **11** There was a man named Lazarus who lived
in the village of Bethany with the two sisters,
² Mary and Martha, and he was ill.—·It was the
same Mary, the sister of the sick man Lazarus,
who anointed the Lord with ointment and wiped
³ his feet with her hair. ·The sisters sent this message to Jesus, "Lord, the man you love is ill."
⁴ On receiving the message, Jesus said, "The sick-
ness will end not in death but in God's glory, and
through it the Son of God will be glorified."

⁵ Jesus loved Martha and her sister and Lazarus,
⁶ yet when he heard that Lazarus was ill he stayed
⁷ where he was for two more days ·before saying to
⁸ the disciples, "Let us go to Judaea." ·The disciples
said, "Rabbi, it is not long since the Jews wanted
⁹ to stone you; are you going back again?" ·Jesus
replied:

"Are there not twelve hours in the day?
A man can walk in the daytime without stum-
   bling
because he has the light of this world to see by;
¹⁰ but if he walks at night he stumbles,
because there is no light to guide him."

¹¹ He said that and then added, "Our friend Laza-

¹² rus is resting, I am going to wake him." ·The disciples said to him, "Lord, if he is able to rest he is
¹³ sure to get better." ·The phrase Jesus used referred to the death of Lazarus, but they thought that by
¹⁴ "rest" he meant "sleep," so ·Jesus put it plainly,
¹⁵ "Lazarus is dead; ·and for your sake I am glad I was not there because now you will believe. But
¹⁶ let us go to him." ·Then Thomas—known as the Twin—said to the other disciples, "Let us go too, and die with him."
¹⁷     On arriving, Jesus found that Lazarus had been
¹⁸ in the tomb for four days already. ·Bethany is only
¹⁹ about two miles from Jerusalem, ·and many Jews had come to Martha and Mary to sympathize with
²⁰ them over their brother. ·When Martha heard that Jesus had come she went to meet him. Mary re-
²¹ mained sitting in the house. ·Martha said to Jesus, "If you had been here, my brother would not have
²² died, ·but I know that, even now, whatever you
²³ ask of God, he will grant you." ·"Your brother,"
²⁴ said Jesus to her, "will rise again." ·Martha said, "I know he will rise again at the resurrection on
²⁵ the last day." ·Jesus said:

"I am the resurrection.
If anyone believes in me, even though he dies
    he will live,
²⁶     and whoever lives and believes in me
    will never die.
Do you believe this?"

²⁷ "Yes, Lord," she said, "I believe that you are the Christ, the Son of God, the one who was to come into this world."
²⁸     When she had said this, she went and called her sister Mary, saying in a low voice, "The Master is
²⁹ here and wants to see you." ·Hearing this, Mary
³⁰ got up quickly and went to him. ·Jesus had not yet come into the village; he was still at the place
³¹ where Martha had met him. ·When the Jews who

were in the house sympathizing with Mary saw
her get up so quickly and go out, they followed
her, thinking that she was going to the tomb to
weep there.

32    Mary went to Jesus, and as soon as she saw him
she threw herself at his feet, saying, "Lord, if you
had been here, my brother would not have died."

33  At the sight of her tears, and those of the Jews
who followed her, Jesus said in great distress,
with a sigh that came straight from the heart,

34  "Where have you put him?" They said, "Lord,
35
36  come and see." ·Jesus wept; ·and the Jews said,
37  "See how much he loved him!" ·But there were
some who remarked, "He opened the eyes of the
blind man, could he not have prevented this man's

38  death?" ·Still sighing, Jesus reached the tomb: it
39  was a cave with a stone to close the opening. ·Jesus
said, "Take the stone away." Martha said to him,
"Lord, by now he will smell; this is the fourth

40  day." ·Jesus replied, "Have I not told you that if
41  you believe you will see the glory of God?" ·So
they took away the stone. Then Jesus lifted up his
eyes and said:

      "Father, I thank you for hearing my prayer.
42    I knew indeed that you always hear me,
       but I speak
       for the sake of all these who stand around me,
       so that they may believe it was you who sent
          me."

43    When he had said this, he cried in a loud voice,
44  "Lazarus, here! Come out!" ·The dead man came
out, his feet and hands bound with bands of stuff
and a cloth around his face. Jesus said to them,
"Unbind him, let him go free."

☩

There are some reasons to think the evangelist added this powerfully told miracle story to his Gospel at a later stage in its composition. It introduces a completely new line of motivation for the passion (in the following section). "The Jews" in this chapter do not show the same hostility to Jesus as elsewhere in the Gospel. In any case, we may be glad he included the story, for it is a masterpiece of his art. He may have had in mind to dramatize Jesus' future eschatological saying about those in the tombs hearing his voice and coming out to resurrection (5:28–29). Symbolically, in the presence of Jesus this is shown to be happening already. More probably the evangelist had in mind to foreshadow the resurrection of Jesus himself, as the hour of the passion, death, and resurrection draws close. Several details of the story have their counterpart in chapter 20.

Is the evangelist a reinterpreter of tradition here also? Very likely he is, but it is difficult to specify the method of his reinterpretation. If he knows the traditions of the Synoptics, in this instance of Luke, we can point to a number of passages that may have influenced him in the Lazarus story. First, there are several stories of the raising of the dead on the part of Jesus, and that is a firm part of the tradition about him. We could single out the restoration to life of the son of the widow of Nain in Luke 7:11–17 as an example. But there is no such story in the Synoptics which is clearly at the root of John's elaborate story. Secondly, for the sisters Martha and Mary one can point to the well-known incident in Luke 10:38–42. The characterization of the two sisters is very close to the picture of them in John 11. Thirdly, there is in Luke the parable of Lazarus and the rich man in heaven and hell (Lk 16:19–31).

This is a parable, not a story about actual persons, but John may have been inspired by it. This becomes an intriguing possibility when one recalls that the parable ends with the rich man saying of his Jewish relatives, "If they will not listen either to Moses or the prophets, they will not be convinced even if someone should rise from the dead." It is quite possible that all these elements were familiar to John in the composition of the Lazarus story.

We cannot comment on every detail of this story, but we may single out a few parts of it for more explanatory remarks. No "sign" in the Fourth Gospel is as clearly interpreted by the evangelist himself as this one is. The long introduction in verses 1–16 contains a good deal of such interpretation, most of it quite clear in its implications. It offers the evangelist another opportunity to use one of his favorite literary devices, that of ambiguity and misunderstanding. Here the problem centers on the language of death, rest, and sleep. The level on which the sign is to be understood, as in the first sign at Cana (2:1–11), is less that of the miraculous than that of the manifestation of divine glory in Jesus (11:4). Thomas—who will reappear prominently in the context of Jesus' own resurrection—is allowed to speak a fine bit of Johannine irony: "Let us go too, and die with him" (verse 16). The question is, with whom? With Jesus, whose life was threatened in Judaea (verse 8), or with Lazarus, who has died (verse 14)? The answer is not obvious, and interpreters have not been unanimous. This is another place at which the reader must decide in light of a general understanding of the Gospel.

Jesus' brief discourse to Martha in verses 25–26 is a famous and deservedly beloved saying. But the inter-

preter must disagree with the JB text. The better
attested evidence of the manuscripts should require us
to read the beginning of the short discourse this way:
"I am the resurrection *and the life*." This enables us to
understand what follows as a comment on each part of
the predicate of the "I am" saying. Jesus is the resurrection, an image central to a future eschatological perspective, in the sense that whoever believes in him,
even after death, will come to life. And he is the (eternal) life, in a realized eschatological perspective, in the
sense that whoever believes in him and possesses eternal life will never die in a definitive sense. The point
may be to assert that whatever are the eschatological
perspectives of the Christian, Jesus is the basis of them.
Martha replies with an impressive christological confession of faith, but her later hesitation at the tomb suggests that even her faith is not yet mature.

The dialogue at the tomb itself (verses 40–42) is a
fine example of how carefully the whole episode is
structured. It deals with believing as a proper response
to a miracle only if the miracle is perceived as a sign of
God's glory. We don't know when Jesus told Martha,
"If you believe you will see the glory of God" (verse
40), but we do know that he has told the reader this
explicitly back in verse 4. Similarly, the ending of
Jesus' prayer in verse 42, "so that they may believe it
was you who sent me," besides being an excellent statement of the purpose of signs in the Gospel, refers back
to Jesus' remark in verse 15.

STUDY QUESTIONS: What kind of eschatological faith
or hope should we have as Chris-
tians? Does it make any difference
to the quality of our lives?

# EVERYBODY WILL BELIEVE IN HIM

⁴⁵ Many of the Jews who had come to visit Mary
⁴⁶ and had seen what he did believed in him, ·but
some of them went to tell the Pharisees what Je-
⁴⁷ sus had done. ·Then the chief priests and Pharisees
called a meeting. "Here is this man working all
these signs," they said, "and what action are we
⁴⁸ taking? ·If we let him go on in this way everybody
will believe in him, and the Romans will come and
⁴⁹ destroy the Holy Place and our nation." ·One of
them, Caiaphas, the high priest that year, said,
"You don't seem to have grasped the situation at
⁵⁰ all; ·you fail to see that it is better for one man
to die for the people, than for the whole nation
⁵¹ to be destroyed." ·He did not speak in his own
person, it was as high priest that he made this
prophecy that Jesus was to die for the nation—
⁵² and not for the nation only, but to gather together
⁵³ in unity the scattered children of God. ·From that
⁵⁴ day they were determined to kill him. ·So Jesus
no longer went about openly among the Jews, but
left the district for a town called Ephraim, in the
country bordering on the desert, and stayed there
with his disciples.

⁵⁵ The Jewish Passover drew near, and many of
the country people who had gone up to Jerusalem
⁵⁶ to purify themselves ·looked out for Jesus, saying

to one another as they stood about in the Temple,
"What do you think? Will he come to the festival
[57] or not?" ·The chief priests and Pharisees had by
now given their orders: anyone who knew where
he was must inform them so that they could arrest
him.

✠

The aftermath of the raising of Lazarus offers the
evangelist an irresistible occasion to display his command of irony as a literary device. Verse 48 is of
course written by and for people who live after the
Roman destruction of Jerusalem and its Temple in A.D.
70. The implication is that what the Pharisees feared
would happen if they let Jesus go on as a messianic
pretender—and thus a threat to Roman order—has in
fact happened anyway. There may even be irony in the
statement that "everybody will believe in him," since
Christianity had in fact spread widely before the time
this Gospel was written. Even more striking irony—to
which the evangelist will refer in a typical cross reference in 18:14—is the "prophecy" of Caiaphas the high
priest, "It is better for one man to die for the people,
than for the whole nation to be destroyed." For the
Christian reader of the Gospel, as indeed for the writer
of it, this becomes an unwitting statement of the saving
character of Jesus' death. But exactly how Jesus' death
was a saving event in the thought of the Fourth Gospel,
we must wait to see.

At this point in the Gospel, the die is cast—or perhaps we should say cast again—and the events of the

passion narrative are imminent. There remain, however, some additional elements of the tradition to be reinterpreted and some concluding reflections of the evangelist for the first part of his Gospel.

# John 12:1–11
## FOR THE DAY OF MY BURIAL

¹ 12 Six days before the Passover, Jesus went to Bethany, where Lazarus was, whom he had ² raised from the dead. ·They gave a dinner for him there; Martha waited on them and Lazarus was ³ among those at table. ·Mary brought in a pound of very costly ointment, pure nard, and with it anointed the feet of Jesus, wiping them with her hair; the house was full of the scent of the oint- ⁴ ment. ·Then Judas Iscariot—one of his disciples, ⁵ the man who was to betray him—said, ·"Why wasn't this ointment sold for three hundred de- ⁶ narii, and the money given to the poor?" ·He said this, not because he cared about the poor, but be- cause he was a thief; he was in charge of the com- mon fund and used to help himself to the contri- ⁷ butions. ·So Jesus said, "Leave her alone; she had ⁸ to keep this scent for the day of my burial. ·You have the poor with you always, you will not al- ways have me."

⁹ Meanwhile a large number of Jews heard that he was there and came not only on account of Jesus but also to see Lazarus whom he had raised ¹⁰ from the dead. ·Then the chief priests decided to ¹¹ kill Lazarus as well, ·since it was on his account that many of the Jews were leaving them and be- lieving in Jesus.

☩

Chapter 12, concluding the Book of Signs, contains a variety of stories, discourses, and reflections, and some of it shows signs of being a collection of materials left over. The first two major incidents are part of the tradition, however, and both are of course reinterpreted.

It is unusually difficult to be precise about just what story John was reinterpreting when he described the anointing of Jesus by Mary of Bethany. In Mark 14:3–9, followed rather closely by Matthew 26:6–13, there is a story of an anointing of Jesus' head by a woman at Bethany. This event just precedes the passion narrative and contains a reference to the burial of Jesus. In Luke 7:36–38 there is a story, unconnected with Bethany or with the passion narrative, in which a woman washes Jesus' feet, dries them with her hair, and anoints them. Two quite separate stories about Jesus underlie these accounts. John knew both, but in exactly what form we are unsure.

What is the point of the story? For John's Gospel, the point is made in verse 7. Mary has performed a symbolic action, almost a prophetic gesture, which calls attention to the death and burial of Jesus. It is not the real anointing of the body for burial; that occurs in 19:39–40. But as a figurative one, it serves to keep our attention focused on the climactic events to come. Mary's gesture was an extravagant one, as the dialogue with Judas the betrayer shows, but conventional values do not apply when Jesus' death is in question. The evangelist sets up a contrast between Judas and Mary that makes the reader all the more aware of the coming passion. Verse 8, which could be a misleading principle if it were taken out of its context and generalized, has to be seen as addressed to the same extraordinary situation of the death of Jesus. If we see it as a reply to Judas, we have to remember that he was not really concerned with the poor anyway (verse 6). But this verse is entirely absent in some important ancient manuscripts, and it may have been inserted by some copyist, taking it from Matthew, in order to harmonize the stories.

Verses 9–11 have no counterpart in the tradition but are a link with the motivation for Jesus' death begun in the Lazarus story. We have no other information anywhere on the plot to kill Lazarus too.

STUDY QUESTION: The great saints of every age have done extravagant things to show their love for God. What kind of extravagance makes sense today?

# John 12:12–19
# THE WHOLE WORLD IS RUNNING AFTER HIM

12 The next day the crowds who had come up for the festival heard that Jesus was on his way to Je-
13 rusalem. ·They took branches of palm and went out to meet him, shouting, "Hosanna! Blessings on the King of Israel, who comes in the name of
14 the Lord." ·Jesus found a young donkey and
15 mounted it—as scripture says: ·Do not be afraid, daughter of Zion; see, your king is coming,
16 mounted on the colt of a donkey. ·At the time his disciples did not understand this, but later, after Jesus had been glorified, they remembered that this had been written about him and that this
17 was in fact how they had received him. ·All who had been with him when he called Lazarus out of the tomb and raised him from the dead were tell-
18 ing how they had witnessed it; ·it was because of this, too, that the crowd came out to meet him:
19 they had heard that he had given this sign. ·Then the Pharisees said to one another, "You see, there is nothing you can do; look, the whole world is running after him!"

✠

The entry of Jesus into Jerusalem is often called the "triumphal entry," but in fact that description may be misleading. Actually, in the quotation from Zechariah 9:9, which is important for the evangelist, the word "triumphant" to describe the entering king is omitted. The point of the story is that the crowd publicly acknowledges Jesus as Messiah, "King of Israel" (see 1:49). But this is a christological faith based at best on signs (verse 18), and ultimately it does not last. Given the generally negative assessment of Jesus' public ministry later in chapter 12, we could call this episode a triumphal entry only in an ironic sense. Of course, with his feeling for irony, the evangelist may have perceived it that way too. The final comment of the Pharisees (verse 19) about the "world" running after Jesus is certainly ironical to the readers of the Gospel.

This passage has numerous points in common with the story of the cleansing of the Temple (2:13–22), and the reader might have another look at the commentary there before proceeding further. Some interpreters think these two stories were closely connected in the tradition upon which John drew, as indeed they are side by side in Mark 11. Like the earlier story, this one centers around Old Testament passages reinterpreted in the light of Jesus. To the words from Psalm 118:25–26 in verse 13 the evangelist has added the phrase "the King of Israel," thus making the quotation explicitly messianic. All four of the Gospel writers quote this passage, with various modifications. The second quotation (verse 15) is a very abbreviated version of Zechariah 9:9. Only Matthew (21:5) actually quotes this verse, in combination with Isaiah 62:11, but there are hints in all the Gospels to suggest the verse was associated with the entry in the pre-Gospel tradition.

Verse 16 explains the process by which the early Christians used the traditions about Jesus and certain passages of the Old Testament to interpret each other. See the commentary on 2:2. The end of verse 16 has a more general application than the JB translation implies. The point is that what was written about Jesus in the Old Testament was what happened to him in fact, and not only the way the crowd received him into the city.

STUDY QUESTION: The early Christians had no hesitation about reading the Old Testament as written about Christ. How far can we go along with them when we read the Old Testament?

## John 12:20–36
# WHO IS THIS SON OF MAN?

<sup>20</sup> Among those who went up to worship at the
<sup>21</sup> festival were some Greeks. ·These approached
Philip, who came from Bethsaida in Galilee, and
put this request to him, "Sir, we should like to
<sup>22</sup> see Jesus." ·Philip went to tell Andrew, and An-
drew and Philip together went to tell Jesus.
<sup>23</sup> Jesus replied to them:

"Now the hour has come
for the Son of Man to be glorified.
<sup>24</sup> I tell you, most solemnly,
unless a wheat grain falls on the ground and
dies,
it remains only a single grain;
but if it dies,
it yields a rich harvest.
<sup>25</sup> Anyone who loves his life loses it;
anyone who hates his life in this world
will keep it for the eternal life.
<sup>26</sup> If a man serves me, he must follow me,
wherever I am, my servant will be there too.
If anyone serves me, my Father will honor him.
<sup>27</sup> Now my soul is troubled.
What shall I say:
Father, save me from this hour?
But it was for this very reason that I have come
to this hour.

28    Father, glorify your name!"

A voice came from heaven, "I have glorified
it, and I will glorify it again."
29    People standing by, who heard this, said it
was a clap of thunder; others said, "It was an
30 angel speaking to him." ·Jesus answered, "It was
not for my sake that this voice came, but for
yours.

31    "Now sentence is being passed on this world;
      now the prince of this world is to be over-
         thrown.
32    And when I am lifted up from the earth,
      I shall draw all men to myself."

33    By these words he indicated the kind of death
34 he would die. ·The crowd answered, "The Law
has taught us that the Christ will remain for ever.
How can you say, 'The Son of Man must be lifted
35 up?' Who is this Son of Man?" ·Jesus then said:

"The light will be with you only a little longer
      now.
Walk while you have the light,
or the dark will overtake you;
he who walks in the dark does not know where
      he is going.
36    While you still have the light,
believe in the light
and you will become sons of light."

Having said this, Jesus left them and kept himself hidden.

✠

The "Greeks" who wanted to see Jesus are most
probably gentiles (as in 7:35) who are already at-

tracted to Judaism and therefore have come there for
the Passover celebration. They provide an occasion for
a discourse of Jesus, but their presence here actually
has a good deal more significance than that. On the
level of the Gospel—as opposed to that of the history of
Jesus—the evangelist is inserting gentiles, who in his
time make up the bulk of the Christian communities,
into the Gospel at the crucial moment when "the hour
has come."

Jesus' discourse in verses 23–32 makes a series of
important statements on the meaning of his death and
on discipleship. In most of it traditional sayings of
Jesus are being extensively reinterpreted. The "hour"
of Jesus (verse 23) in the Johannine vocabulary is the
time of the passion, which, also in the Johannine vocabulary, is the "glorification" of Jesus. We have seen
that this hour has been spoken of as future, but it could
be anticipated when Jesus manifested his glory in signs
(see, e.g., the first Cana story, 2:1–11). The coming of
the hour will be solemnly announced when the passion
narrative begins in 13:1, but here it is proclaimed by
Jesus again in an anticipatory manner. It is possible
that a similarly special use of the word "hour" was already in the passion tradition, for we find it used twice
in Mark's account of the agony in the garden (Mk
14:32–42).

Verse 27 shows us John's reinterpretation of that
scene in the garden. With its emphasis on Jesus as divine, the Fourth Gospel does not portray him as praying for deliverance from the impending suffering which
he clearly foresees. Instead, he rejects the thought of
such a prayer and calls upon God to fulfill the process
of glorification, which of course involves Jesus' own

death. The divine voice with its solemn utterance lends an awesome supernatural tone to the coming events. The "thunder" is an ancient religious symbol, in the Bible as well as in many other religious traditions, for the voice of God. Though ambiguous in itself, it does not mean here simply that people completely mistook the words for mere thunder.

The solemn tone continues as Jesus places the passion in a cosmic context in which "the prince of this world," the devil as embodiment of opposition to God, is to be overthrown. The context is also an appropriate one for the third prediction of the passion, the "lifting up" of Jesus. As we know from a cross reference to come in 18:32, this indicates that the "lifting up" means hanging on the cross, a Roman form of execution as opposed to a Jewish execution by stoning, if indeed that was legal. Verse 32 does not mention the Son of Man, which is a firm part of the tradition of the passion predictions, but the question of the crowd in verse 34 serves to bring the prediction into line with the others. To the extent that the fragment of discourse in verses 35–36 may be considered an answer to the question "Who is this Son of Man?" it is a beautiful recapitulation of the light-darkness theme in christological terms. The light and the dark, alternative symbols to the above and the below, the truth and the lie, and other contrasts, align the Son of Man with the world of God appearing in the world of humanity.

STUDY QUESTIONS: In our age, when the value of life is strongly affirmed though not always respected, how shall we understand the saying of Jesus in verse 25? What does it mean to a world that is increasingly less dualistic to speak of "walking in the light" rather than in the darkness?

# THEY DID NOT BELIEVE IN HIM

37 38   Though they had been present when he gave so many signs, they did not believe in him; ·this was to fulfill the words of the prophet Isaiah: Lord, who could believe what we have heard said, and to whom has the power of the Lord been re-

39 40   vealed? ·Indeed, they were unable to believe because, as Isaiah says again: ·He has blinded their eyes, he has hardened their heart, for fear they should see with their eyes and understand with their heart, and turn to me for healing.

41   Isaiah said this when he saw his glory, and his words referred to Jesus.

42   And yet there were many who did believe in him, even among the leading men, but they did not admit it, through fear of the Pharisees and

43   fear of being expelled from the synagogue: ·they put honor from men before the honor that comes from God.

44   Jesus declared publicly:

"Whoever believes in me
believes not in me
but in the one who sent me,

45   and whoever sees me,
sees the one who sent me.

46     I, the light, have come into the world,
     so that whoever believes in me
     need not stay in the dark any more.
47     If anyone hears my words and does not keep
       them faithfully,
     it is not I who shall condemn him,
     since I have come not to condemn the world,
     but to save the world:
48     he who rejects me and refuses my words
     has his judge already:
     the word itself that I have spoken
     will be his judge on the last day.
49     For what I have spoken does not come from
       myself;
     no, what I was to say, what I had to speak,
     was commanded by the Father who sent me,
50     and I know that his commands mean eternal
       life.
     And therefore what the Father has told me
     is what I speak."

☩

There are really two conclusions to the Book of Signs, one a rather negative reflection of the evangelist on the results (verses 37–43), the other a discourse of Jesus which functions as a summary of his discourses and also has a prominent negative side to it (verses 44–50). For the negativism of the evangelist's reflections we need to recall the prologue, 1:11: "He came to his own domain and his own people did not accept him." John describes here two classes of people whose response was inadequate. Those who, in spite of the many signs, simply did not come to any kind of faith in Jesus—"the Jews" in the Johannine usage. Second, the cryptobelievers, those who came to a certain level of belief, including some "leading men" among the Jews (Nicodemus among others?), but whose faith was not strong enough to permit them to suffer the consequences, as the man born blind had done. The force of John's scathing description of the latter group is more effective when we realize that the word translated "honor" in verse 43 is the same as that for "glory" throughout the Gospel. Both groups of people are of course not only characters in the story but contemporaries of the evangelist and his church.

The description of the unbelievers centers around two quotations from Isaiah which were both used in early Christianity to explain the fact that most Jews had not actually accepted Jesus as Messiah and thus become Christians. The first is also used by Paul in Romans 10:16, and for a purpose similar to John's. The second is used in the other Gospels and in the Acts of the Apostles (see Ac 28:25–27). To see how this theme of fulfillment of prophecy is used, we must recall that the given is the fact that the Jews have not believed. A biblical explanation of the fact is then brought forward. Deterministic as it sounds, the evangelist did not really believe they had no choice in the matter. For the fourth evangelist, Isaiah, like Moses in the Law (see 5:46), was writing about the time of Jesus.

The summary discourse of Jesus is, from the point of view of the story, a misfit. In 12:36 Jesus had formally withdrawn, to reappear again in the passion narrative after the introduction to the second part of the Gospel. But here he cries out like a voice from the wings of the stage. The discourse, which is almost totally repetition of discourse themes and phrases used before, is not inappropriate as a summary on the literary level, however. We cannot tell whether the evangelist composed it for this purpose or he simply had it left over from a larger collection of discourses. While the role of Jesus' words in provoking judgment is very prominent in it, the main focus is still on Christology and the relationship of the Son to the Father.

STUDY QUESTIONS: What should be the Christian's attitude toward those who do not enjoy the gift of faith? Do we detect levels of faith in ourselves and in others? Can a contemporary Christian, who deals with the whole Bible, not just with the Fourth Gospel, afford to draw the lines of belief as sharply as John does?

*The Book of Glory*
John 13:1 to 20:31

## Introduction to John 13:1 to 20:31
# THE BOOK OF GLORY

Now that we have become familiar with John's associa-
tion of the terms "glory" and "glorification" with the
death and resurrection of Jesus, it seems appropriate to
adopt Raymond E. Brown's name for the second major
division of the Gospel. We might recall that though a
very formal beginning in chapter 13 marks a new major
section, the more important principle of division is the
audience Jesus addresses and the consequent tone of
his address. From this point on, Jesus' discourses are
spoken to the disciples, to those who despite their im-
perfect understanding of what they have heard and
seen, nevertheless have declined to "go away" (6:67).
And the content of Jesus' message changes also. It now
becomes a message about love—the love of the Father
and the Son for each other and of both for the disciples, who are given the new commandment to love each
other. And the death of Jesus, which is of course central to any Gospel, is the revelation of a love than
which there is none greater (see 15:13).

There are four major sections of the Book of Glory,
and in them the reinterpretative hand of the evangelist
continues to be prominent. First, there is the account of

the Last Supper (13:1–38), which is radically different
from its synoptic counterpart, and therefore presumably from the tradition the evangelist used. Instead of
the story of the institution of the Eucharist, which is
dominant in the Synoptics, there is a story about footwashing, about which the other Gospels know nothing.
Certain other episodes are common to John and the
Synoptics, however, as we shall see.

Secondly, the very long discourse—perhaps better,
collection of discourses—which John places after the
Supper is an almost completely original feature of the
Fourth Gospel (14:1 to 17:26). At the most this passage reinterprets some sayings of Jesus from the tradition, but there are few close ties. It has little or nothing
in common with the discourse of Jesus *before* the passion in the Synoptics (see, e.g., Mk 13). To understand
the Johannine discourse adequately, we must realize
that it is a kind of commentary, in anticipation, on the
passion and resurrection narratives. Ideally the student
of this Gospel should reread the discourse after reading
what follows it. The discourse is often appropriately
called Jesus' "farewell discourse." From the point of
view of ancient literature, it has several resemblances to
the "testament," the farewell message and spiritual leg-
acy of a dying religious figure.

Thirdly, the passion narrative itself narrates the
events from the arrest of Jesus to his burial (18:1 to
19:42). We shall note many details of similarity and
difference with respect to the synoptic accounts. The
Johannine story accentuates the autonomy of Jesus in
the passion. He lays down his life; it is not just taken
from him. In fact, he behaves throughout almost as the
architect of the passion, not its victim. He is the Son of
God dying out of love for his friends. The focal point

of this section of the book is obviously the trial before
Pilate, which the evangelist has expanded greatly beyond the rather obscure traditional data and to which
he has devoted some of his most powerful literary
talent.

The resurrection stories (20:1–29) include both the
empty tomb and several appearances of the risen Jesus.
But here, as a more detailed examination will show,
there is a great deal of reinterpretation along the lines
of Johannine theology. It is not the resurrection as such
that is important for John, but its value in showing
Jesus' fidelity to his promises to the disciples.

## John 13:1–20
## NO SERVANT IS GREATER THAN
## HIS MASTER

¹ 13 It was before the festival of the Passover, and Jesus knew that the hour had come for him to pass from this world to the Father. He had always loved those who were his in the world, but now he showed how perfect his love was.

² They were at supper, and the devil had already put it into the mind of Judas Iscariot son of Simon,
³ to betray him. ·Jesus knew that the Father had put everything into his hands, and that he had come
⁴ from God and was returning to God, ·and he got up from table, removed his outer garment and,
⁵ taking a towel, wrapped it around his waist; ·he then poured water into a basin and began to wash the disciples' feet and to wipe them with the towel he was wearing.

⁶ He came to Simon Peter, who said to him,
⁷ "Lord, are you going to wash my feet?" ·Jesus answered, "At the moment you do not know what I am doing, but later you will understand."
⁸ "Never!" said Peter. "You shall never wash my feet." Jesus replied, "If I do not wash you, you
⁹ can have nothing in common with me." ·"Then, Lord," said Simon Peter, "not only my feet, but
¹⁰ my hands and my head as well!" ·Jesus said, "No

one who has taken a bath needs washing, he is clean all over. You too are clean, though not all

11 of you are." ·He knew who was going to betray him, that was why he said, "though not all of you are."

12 When he had washed their feet and put on his clothes again he went back to the table. "Do you understand," he said, "what I have done to you?

13 You call me Master and Lord, and rightly; so I

14 am. ·If I, then, the Lord and Master, have washed

15 your feet, you should wash each other's feet. ·I have given you an example so that you may copy what I have done to you.

16 "I tell you most solemnly,
     no servant is greater than his master,
     no messenger is greater than the man who sent
       him.

17 "Now that you know this, happiness will be

18 yours if you behave accordingly. ·I am not speaking about all of you: I know the ones I have chosen; but what scripture says must be fulfilled: Someone who shares my table rebels against me.

19 "I tell you this now, before it happens,
     so that when it does happen
     you may believe that I am He.

20 I tell you most solemnly,
     whoever welcomes the one I send welcomes me,
     and whoever welcomes me welcomes the one
       who sent me."

✠

The Book of Glory begins with a very solemn style that is somewhat unusual for John. Verse 1 in Greek is a single sentence, the end of which could also—and perhaps better—be translated: "he loved them to the end." If we understand "to the end" as "until death," which is a possible meaning of the phrase, then the statement makes a good introduction to the whole Book of Glory as well as to the Last Supper. It anticipates the interpretation of Jesus' death as an act of love. Love is introduced somewhat abruptly here, but the discourses to follow will explain it fully.

As usual in the Fourth Gospel, the time is indicated in relation to a festival of the Jewish calendar. This time, however, it poses a special problem. In the Synoptic Gospels the Last Supper is not *before* the Passover but is the festive Passover meal itself, celebrated in the evening after sundown when the feast begins. Even though the Eucharist is not mentioned, the meal here is the same one, as the references to the betrayal by Judas and the prediction of Peter's denials (see next section) show. Are the discrepancies in date reconcilable?

The efforts of interpreters to reconcile them have not proved successful. The most promising suggestion in recent years has centered on evidence that two different Jewish calendars existed in Palestine in Jesus' time, but it has not been shown that Jesus and official Judaism were at variance on this point. Instead of a historical solution, we must seek a theological one. For the synoptic writers, the Passover symbolism is localized in the Eucharist, which is understood as the Christian Passover celebration. This emphasis necessitates seeing the Last Supper as the Passover and following out the passion chronology accordingly. For John the Eucharist is absent, and the Passover symbolism is applied to Jesus himself, whose death takes place in the afternoon before the Passover meal, at the same time the sacrificial

lambs are slaughtered in the temple. It is no longer possible to determine which tradition is historically more
accurate. The important thing is that we do not let curiosity about the historicity blind us to the theological
symbolism in all the Gospels.

Verses 2–4 also form a single sentence in Greek,
combining practical details with a sweeping christological perspective. More than in other accounts of the
Last Supper, the betrayal of Jesus by Judas has an
overshadowing presence at the Supper. Besides being
foretold a number of times in the Book of Signs, as we
have seen, it figures prominently here in verses 2, 11,
and 18 (where it is interpreted by Ps 41:9), even
though it will not be dealt with formally until the next
section. The emphasis is all the more remarkable when
we realize that in the garden scene Jesus confronts his
accusers on his own initiative and there is hardly a role
for Judas to play (see 18:2–5). Perhaps the reason for
stressing the betrayal is to provide a foil for interpreting
Jesus' death as an act of love. Betrayal on the part of a
trusted disciple not only contrasts with Jesus' own attitude but makes it all the more powerful.

The footwashing is an act of humility, to be sure—the
contrast between the roles of servant and master implies this. But one may question whether humility,
which is not mentioned as such, is the main emphasis of
the story. Actually, two explanations of the action of
Jesus are present in the text. The first, in verses 6–11,
demands the disciples' participation in the gesture of
Jesus. The Christian tradition has turned to baptism to
interpret the event, but not every mention of water is
baptismal. Jesus' action may be another prophetic gesture, somehow pointing toward his death, in which his

followers must share as beneficiaries of his love for his
friends.

The second explanation is in any event clearer
(verses 12–20). In it Jesus defines his authority as
Lord and Master in terms of performing an act of service, even the menial service associated with the lowest
household slave. And he commands his followers to
copy his example. The Fourth Gospel has little to say
about practical life in the church, but it seems here to
convey an important statement about leadership and
authority in the church, namely that it is to be exercised in service as Jesus served his disciples. Jesus' ultimate act of service was his death.

The brief discourse at the end of the section provides
another occasion for an "I am" saying which lacks any
predicate in the context. It suggests that when Jesus is
betrayed, that is in his death, his divine identity will appear.

STUDY QUESTION: For centuries the church has interpreted verse 14 literally by cele-
brating the *mandatum* on Maundy
Thursday, by a liturgical footwashing. How should we evaluate
this practice in the light of John's
Gospel?

## John 13:21–38
## NIGHT HAS FALLEN

21    Having said this, Jesus was troubled in spirit
and declared, "I tell you most solemnly, one of
22 you will betray me." ·The disciples looked at one
23 another, wondering which he meant. ·The disciple
24 Jesus loved was reclining next to Jesus; ·Simon
Peter signed to him and said, "Ask who it is he
25 means," ·so leaning back on Jesus' breast he said,
26 "Who is it, Lord?" ·"It is the one," replied Jesus,
"to whom I give the piece of bread that I shall dip
in the dish." He dipped the piece of bread and
27 gave it to Judas son of Simon Iscariot. ·At that
instant, after Judas had taken the bread, Satan entered him. Jesus then said, "What you are going
28 to do, do quickly." ·None of the others at table
29 understood the reason he said this. ·Since Judas
had charge of the common fund, some of them
thought Jesus was telling him, "Buy what we need
for the festival," or telling him to give something
30 to the poor. ·As soon as Judas had taken the piece
of bread he went out. Night had fallen.
31    When he had gone Jesus said:

"Now has the Son of Man been glorified,
and in him God has been glorified.
32 If God has been glorified in him,
God will in turn glorify him in himself,
and will glorify him very soon.

33    "My little children,
      I shall not be with you much longer.
      You will look for me,
      and, as I told the Jews,
      where I am going,
      you cannot come.
34    I give you a new commandment:
      love one another;
      just as I have loved you,
      you also must love one another.
35    By this love you have for one another,
      everyone will know that you are my disciples."

36    Simon Peter said, "Lord, where are you going?"
      Jesus replied, "Where I am going you cannot
37    follow me now; you will follow me later." ·Peter
      said to him, "Why can't I follow you now? I will
38    lay down my life for you." ·"Lay down your life
      for me?" answered Jesus. "I tell you most sol-
      emnly, before the cock crows you will have dis-
      owned me three times.

✠

The division between the Last Supper narrative and
the farewell discourses is not a neat and clear-cut one.
Verses 21–38 are grouped together here because the
prediction of Peter's denial at the end of the chapter is
traditionally connected with the Last Supper story (see
Lk 22:31–34). But the discourses actually begin with
13:33 or even with 13:31.

The story of the departure of Judas mingles the inti-
macy of the Supper with the cosmic implications of
Satan entering into Judas. And with typical Johannine
emphasis on the theme of misunderstanding, the other
disciples are unaware of the real drama. But unlike the

disciples in the Markan account, they do not doubt
their own loyalty. The evangelist ends the narrative
with consummate dramatic effect by the simple remark
"Night had fallen" (verse 30), which recalls 9:4: "The
night will soon be here when no one can work." In
Luke 22:53 Jesus says to those who have come to arrest him: "But this is your hour; this is the reign of
darkness."

The account of the betrayer introduces for the first
time "the disciple Jesus loved," who enjoys a position
close to Jesus at the Supper. An ancient tradition
identifies this personage of the Gospel with John the
apostle, and one can neither prove nor disprove it. The
Gospel itself suggests that this disciple is the authority
for the tradition contained in it, if, as is likely, the same
person is meant in 19:35. The appendix explicitly
states the Johannine church's confidence in his testimony (21:24). Yet some have argued that the beloved
disciple is not meant to be a real person but a symbol
of the true Johannine believer who is close to Jesus and
who testifies to the traditions about him. Perhaps it is
not essential to choose between these options. The disciple who was at the root of the peculiarly Johannine
understanding of Jesus may indeed have been thought
of as a model for the Christian believer.

Jesus gives a "new commandment" of mutual love,
about which we shall hear more in the discourses to
follow. In view of the fact that the Old Testament had
enjoined love of one's neighbor (Lv 19:18, often repeated in the Synoptics and in Paul), one may ask what
is "new" about Jesus' commandment. The answer is
not obvious, but we may suggest that the newness lies
in the analogy with Jesus' own love: "Just as I have
loved you, you also must love one another" (verse

34). It is often pointed out that in the Fourth Gospel love is not as demanding or as characteristically Christian as elsewhere in the New Testament. It is only love for one another, not love of neighbor in general, much less love of enemies as in the Sermon on the Mount. Yet if its specificity is that it is love *as Jesus loved,* then it does have a radical dimension, for Jesus' love was ultimately the laying down of his life (see 15:13). We shall see the same point made repeatedly in the discourses to come, with constant emphasis on the love of the Son and the Father.

The prediction of Peter's denial, with which the reader is familiar from the synoptic Last Supper accounts, offers the evangelist another opportunity for irony: Peter is willing to "lay down his life for" Jesus—the formula is the same as Jesus uses in 15:13. He will indeed do so, as the appendix reminds us (21:18), but not before he experiences the denial.

STUDY QUESTION: The Fourth Gospel offers few details about what Christian love consists in. How should we flesh out this new commandment in practice?

# John 14:1–31
## IF YOU KNOW ME,
## YOU KNOW MY FATHER TOO

**1** **14** "Do not let your hearts be troubled.
Trust in God still, and trust in me.

**2**   There are many rooms in my Father's house;
if there were not, I should have told you.
I am going now to prepare a place for you,

**3**   and after I have gone and prepared you a place,
I shall return to take you with me;
so that where I am
you may be too.

**4**   You know the way to the place where I am
going."

**5**   Thomas said, "Lord, we do not know where
you are going, so how can we know the way?"
**6** Jesus said:

"I am the Way, the Truth and the Life.
No one can come to the Father except through
me.

**7**   If you know me, you know my Father too.
From this moment you know him and have
seen him."

**8**   Philip said, "Lord, let us see the Father and then
**9** we shall be satisfied." ·"Have I been with you all
this time, Philip," said Jesus to him, "and you
still do not know me?

"To have seen me is to have seen the Father,
so how can you say, 'Let us see the Father?'

10  Do you not believe
that I am in the Father and the Father is in me?
The words I say to you I do not speak as from
   myself:
it is the Father, living in me, who is doing this
   work.

11  You must believe me when I say
that I am in the Father and the Father is in me;
believe it on the evidence of this work, if for no
   other reason.

12  I tell you most solemnly,
whoever believes in me
will perform the same works as I do myself,
he will perform even greater works,
because I am going to the Father.

13  Whatever you ask for in my name I will do,
so that the Father may be glorified in the Son.

14  If you ask for anything in my name,
I will do it.

15  If you love me you will keep my commandments.

16  I shall ask the Father,
and he will give you another Advocate
to be with you for ever,

17  that Spirit of truth
whom the world can never receive
since it neither sees nor knows him;
but you know him,
because he is with you, he is in you.

18  I will not leave you orphans;
I will come back to you.

19  In a short time the world will no longer see me;
but you will see me,
because I live and you will live.

20  On that day
you will understand that I am in my Father
and you in me and I in you.

21  Anybody who receives my commandments and
        keeps them
    will be one who loves me;
    and anybody who loves me will be loved by my
        Father,
    and I shall love him and show myself to him."

22  Judas—this was not Judas Iscariot—said to him,
    "Lord, what is all this about? Do you intend to
23  show yourself to us and not to the world?" ·Jesus
    replied:

    "If anyone loves me he will keep my word,
    and my Father will love him,
    and we shall come to him
    and make our home with him.
24  Those who do not love me do not keep my
        words.
    And my word is not my own:
    it is the word of the one who sent me.
25  I have said these things to you
    while still with you;
26  but the Advocate, the Holy Spirit,
    whom the Father will send in my name,
    will teach you everything
    and remind you of all I have said to you.
27  Peace I bequeath to you,
    my own peace I give you,
    a peace the world cannot give, this is my gift
        to you.
    Do not let your hearts be troubled or afraid.
28  You heard me say:
    I am going away, and shall return.
    If you loved me you would have been glad to
        know that I am going to the Father,
    for the Father is greater than I.
29  I have told you this now before it happens,
    so that when it does happen you may believe.
30  I shall not talk with you any longer,
    because the prince of this world is on his way.
    He has no power over me,

31      but the world must be brought to know that I
            love the Father
        and that I am doing exactly what the Father
            told me.
        Come now, let us go.

☩

The farewell discourses (13:33 to 17:26) are not
unified in form or in content, most probably because
they consist of various originally distinct portions of
discourse. Chapter 14 alerts us to this problem in that
it is complete in itself, ending with what appears to be a
final remark by Jesus. Yet there are three more chapters of discourse to follow. The result of this collection
is a very long section characterized by repetition, variations on the same themes, sometimes even contradiction. But there is an overall unity of themes
throughout the chapters, such as the departure and return of Jesus, the sending of the Holy Spirit, the mutual
love of Father and Son, the new commandment of love,
and others.

What is most distinctive about these discourses, however, is the tone of them. There is none of the air of
confrontation and challenge that marked the discourses
of the Book of Signs. Even the use of symbols and misunderstanding is greatly lessened, though Jesus does
not speak quite as plainly as the disciples exuberantly
exclaim in 16:29. What accounts for the change in tone
is that these discourses are addressed to the disciples—
and thus to the Christian readers of the Gospel—to help
them interpret the death and resurrection of Jesus. It is
hard to discover logical patterns which would enable us

to divide the discourses into smaller units, and perhaps
we are not meant to. We shall comment on them, therefore, in large blocks, calling attention to only some of
the recurrent themes. Chapters 14 and 16 have several
questions or remarks of the disciples, but these scarcely
interrupt the flow of the discourse.

Because the discourses comment on events yet to
happen, time is as it were collapsed in them. Present,
past, and future are not logically distinct. Verse 25 is a
good indication of this, for Jesus speaks as though he
had already departed.

The emphasis of the discourse in chapter 14 and indeed of the others also is on the consequences for the
disciples of Jesus' return to the Father. But the discourses continue to be christologically oriented, particularly in terms of Jesus' relationship to the Father.
Such statements as "If you know me, you know my Father too" and "To have seen me is to have seen the Father" (verses 7, 9) are some of the strongest assertions
in the Gospel that Jesus is the revelation of God himself. In Johannine thought it is this primary role of
Jesus as revealer which undergirds the exclusive claim
of Jesus to be not only the Way to the Father but the
only way to him (verse 6). Despite the lofty claims of
Jesus to be the revelation of the Father, the Fourth
Gospel does not simply equate Jesus with God. Jesus
and the Father are mutually in each other (verse 11),
yet Jesus must go to the Father, "for the Father is
greater than I" (verse 28).

One of Jesus' main purposes in this discourse is to
instruct the disciples to carry on his mission in the
world after his departure to the Father. They are to
"perform the same works" as he, even greater ones
(verse 12). Our acquaintance with Johannine vocabu-

lary enables us to translate this task as to confront the world with the revealing word of God and thus bring people to faith. But the disciples, who lack understanding, are bewildered, and are even about to desert Jesus in his passion, can hardly carry out this mission unaided. Hence Jesus promises them the Holy Spirit of truth who will be with them forever.

Verses 16–17 and 26 are the first two of several passages promising that the Father (or Jesus) will send the Advocate, the Holy Spirit. This designation of the Holy Spirit is unique in the Fourth Gospel (and the First Epistle of John) and obscure in its origin. It may be preferable to use the word "Paraclete," however, which is merely taking over the Greek word used, since such translations as "Advocate" and "Counselor" indicate only limited aspects of what the Paraclete is to do for the church. The most important point to note is that this is *another* Paraclete (verse 16), implying that Jesus has fulfilled the same role while he was with the disciples. The Holy Spirit, therefore, in this capacity is the continued divine presence assisting the disciples to perform the mission of Jesus in the world. He will remain with them and within them. He will teach them everything and make them remember all that Jesus has said (see the comment on 2:22). The Fourth Gospel itself is thus evidence of the work of the Paraclete in the Johannine church.

STUDY QUESTIONS: What do we learn about God if the ultimate revelation of him is in the human Jesus? How does the Spirit function as a Paraclete (advocate, counselor, instructor) in the church of today?

## John 15:1–17
## I AM THE VINE

<sup>1</sup> **15** "I am the true vine,
and my Father is the vinedresser.
<sup>2</sup> Every branch in me that bears no fruit
he cuts away,
and every branch that does bear fruit he prunes
to make it bear even more.
<sup>3</sup> You are pruned already,
by means of the word that I have spoken to you.
<sup>4</sup> Make your home in me, as I make mine in you.
As a branch cannot bear fruit all by itself,
but must remain part of the vine,
neither can you unless you remain in me.
<sup>5</sup> I am the vine,
you are the branches.
Whoever remains in me, with me in him,
bears fruit in plenty;
for cut off from me you can do nothing.
<sup>6</sup> Anyone who does not remain in me
is like a branch that has been thrown away
—he withers;
these branches are collected and thrown on the
fire,
and they are burned.
<sup>7</sup> If you remain in me
and my words remain in you,

you may ask what you will
and you shall get it.

8 It is to the glory of my Father that you should
    bear much fruit,
and then you will be my disciples.

9 As the Father has loved me,
so I have loved you.
Remain in my love.

10 If you keep my commandments
you will remain in my love,
just as I have kept my Father's commandments
and remain in his love.

11 I have told you this
so that my own joy may be in you
and your joy be complete.

12 This is my commandment:
love one another,
as I have loved you.

13 A man can have no greater love
than to lay down his life for his friends.

14 You are my friends,
if you do what I command you.

15 I shall not call you servants any more,
because a servant does not know
his master's business;
I call you friends,
because I have made known to you
everything I have learned from my Father.

16 You did not choose me,
no, I chose you;
and I commissioned you
to go out and to bear fruit,
fruit that will last;
and then the Father will give you
anything you ask him in my name.

17 What I command you
is to love one another.

✠

A new section of the farewell discourses, or perhaps a new discourse in the collection, begins very abruptly with a predicative "I am" saying and introduces a new symbol. We have the feeling that we are suddenly brought into a discussion—about a vine or at least a vineyard, presumably—that has been going on already. That is to say that the extended figure of speech here (compare the use of pastoral imagery in chapter 10) seems to be a commentary on something—a parable? a metaphor?—but we cannot say on what. The technique is allegorical: Jesus identifies the vine, the vinedresser, the branches, dead branches, and (implicitly) the fruit.

Symbolism involving vines and vineyards can be found extensively in the Old Testament (e.g., Is 5:1–7; Ezk 17; Ps 80:8–16; etc.) and in some parables in the gospel tradition (e.g., Mk 12:1–11, etc.), but it can also be found in pagan religious traditions. No specific background for John's imagery here has been convincingly demonstrated, and perhaps we should regard the vine symbol on a par with many of the other Johannine symbols such as water, bread, light, and the rest. They are chosen because their value as religious symbols is widespread—perhaps, in the experience of the evangelist, universal. Biblical backgrounds are not excluded, but are not exclusive either.

For some interpreters, ancient and modern, the vine symbol has eucharistic significance, suggested partly by the connection between the farewell discourses and the Last Supper account. In the Markan account of the Supper Jesus says, "I shall not drink any more of the fruit of the vine [JB: any more wine] until that day when I drink it anew in the kingdom of God" (Mk 14:25). But the image in John 15 does not mention wine, only the vine, the branches, and the fruit, and

John displays no interest in the Eucharist at the Last Supper.

Similarly, we should be hesitant to speak of imagery of the church here. There is no hint of the collective relationship of the branches to the vine, but rather of the individual, personal relationship of the disciples to Jesus as the source of their life. Such an emphasis is characteristic of the Fourth Gospel and should neither be subordinated nor preferred to other images of Christian life in the New Testament. They all have their contribution to make to Christian theology and self-understanding.

All questions of background aside, the passage is an eloquent expression of the relationship of the believer to Christ and of the meaning of the commandment of love. Here the commandment is rooted in the mutual love of Father and Son and the mutual love of Jesus and the disciples. The theme of mutuality, or reciprocity, of love has its almost mystical counterpart in the notion of mutual indwelling of Father, Son, and disciples. Love of Christians for one another is for John but a reflection of love at much deeper levels.

STUDY QUESTION: Obviously Christian faith and love cannot be merely an individual matter. How then should one express the importance of individual relationship to Christ in a modern, socially oriented church?

## John 15:18 to 16:4a
# THEY HATED ME FOR NO REASON

18     "If the world hates you,
      remember that it hated me before you.
19     If you belonged to the world,
      the world would love you as its own;
      but because you do not belong to the world,
      because my choice withdrew you from the
         world,
      therefore the world hates you.
20     Remember the words I said to you:
      A servant is not greater than his master.
      If they persecuted me,
      they will persecute you too;
      if they kept my word,
      they will keep yours as well.
21     But it will be on my account that they will do
         all this,
      because they do not know the one who sent me.
22     If I had not come,
      if I had not spoken to them,
      they would have been blameless;
      but as it is they have no excuse for their sin.
23     Anyone who hates me hates my Father.
24     If I had not performed such works among them
      as no one else has ever done,
      they would be blameless;

but as it is, they have seen all this,
and still they hate both me and my Father.

25 But all this was only to fulfill the words written
in their Law:
They hated me for no reason.

26 When the Advocate comes,
whom I shall send to you from the Father,
the Spirit of truth who issues from the Father,
he will be my witness.

27 And you too will be witnesses,
because you have been with me from the outset.

1 **16** I have told you all this
so that your faith may not be shaken.

2 They will expel you from the synagogues,
and indeed the hour is coming
when anyone who kills you will think he is doing a holy duty for God.

3 They will do these things
because they have never known either the Father or myself.

4 But I have told you all this,
so that when the time for it comes
you may remember that I told you.

✠

The theme of this section of the discourse is that of
incomprehension, opposition, and finally persecution
on the part of "the world." And throughout, the analogy is drawn between the way the world has treated,
and in the passion will treat, Jesus and the way it will
treat the believers in Jesus. The statement of 13:16
that "no servant is greater than his master" is reinterpreted here to mean that if the master was not im-
mune from persecution, neither will the servants be
(verse 20).

The Fourth Gospel uses the word "world" extremely frequently and in its own distinctive but not quite uniform way. It does not mean simply material creation as opposed to spiritual reality. If it is proper to speak of dualism in John, it is not a gnostic type of dualism. For John, the world means the world of people, something close to the term "mankind." Jesus' mission is to be Savior of the world (4:42) and light of the world (8:12) because the Father loved the world (3:16). But in a majority of cases in the Gospel, and increasingly in the latter half of it, "the world" is used in a pejorative sense for those who reject faith in Jesus, who oppose and persecute him and his followers. The world in this sense is dominated by Satan, "the prince of this world" (14:30), and Jesus must conquer it (16:33). Especially in the prayer of Jesus in chapter 17 the lines are drawn sharply between the disciples of Jesus and the world.

The Johannine church experiences opposition from outside itself and defines its experience in the radically opposing poles of God vs. world. It is clear from verse 25, which cites Psalm 35:19 or 69:4, that "the world" for this church is virtually equivalent to "the Jews." The opening verses of chapter 16 remind us for a third time that what is at issue is expulsion of the Christians from the synagogue. Jesus' words predict not only such an expulsion but even the killing of Christians. It is hard to say whether there actually was such violent persecution of Christians in the experience of the Johannine community, but they are encouraged to be prepared for it.

The Paraclete is mentioned in this discourse also (15:26–27), and this time his role is to bear witness to Jesus in the presence of a hostile world, as Jesus himself did in the polemical discourses of the Book of Signs. Actually the witnessing function is to be that of the disciples, but it is the Spirit who will empower them to carry it out.

This discourse also ends with a note of finality in the first half of 16:4, but another discourse follows with no new introduction.

STUDY QUESTIONS: How does the modern Christian experience the world? Is it necessary, or even proper, for modern Christians to adopt the Johannine attitude toward the world?

## John 16:4b–33
# YOUR SORROW WILL TURN TO JOY

"I did not tell you this from the outset,
because I was with you;

5 but now I am going to the one who sent me.
Not one of you has asked, 'Where are you
going?'

6 Yet you are sad at heart because I have told you
this.

7 Still, I must tell you the truth:
it is for your own good that I am going
because unless I go,
the Advocate will not come to you;
but if I do go,
I will send him to you.

8 And when he comes,
he will show the world how wrong it was,
about sin,
and about who was in the right,
and about judgment:

9 about sin:
proved by their refusal to believe in me;

10 about who was in the right:
proved by my going to the Father
and your seeing me no more;

11 about judgment:
proved by the prince of this world being already
condemned.

12    I still have many things to say to you
but they would be too much for you now.

13    But when the Spirit of truth comes
he will lead you to the complete truth,
since he will not be speaking as from himself
but will say only what he has learned;
and he will tell you of the things to come.

14    He will glorify me,
since all he tells you
will be taken from what is mine.

15    Everything the Father has is mine;
that is why I said:
All he tells you
will be taken from what is mine.

16    "In a short time you will no longer see me,
and then a short time later you will see me
again."

17    Then some of his disciples said to one another,
"What does he mean, 'In a short time you will no
longer see me, and then a short time later you
will see me again' and, 'I am going to the Father'?
18 What is this 'short time'? We don't know what he
19 means." ·Jesus knew that they wanted to question
him, so he said, "You are asking one another what
I meant by saying: In a short time you will no
longer see me, and then a short time later you will
see me again.

20    "I tell you most solemnly,
you will be weeping and wailing
while the world will rejoice;
you will be sorrowful,
but your sorrow will turn to joy.

21    A woman in childbirth suffers,
because her time has come;
but when she has given birth to the child she
forgets the suffering
in her joy that a man has been born into the
world.

22    So it is with you: you are sad now,
      but I shall see you again, and your hearts will
          be full of joy,
      and that joy no one shall take from you.
23    When that day comes,
      you will not ask me any questions.
      I tell you most solemnly,
      anything you ask for from the Father
      he will grant in my name.
24    Until now you have not asked for anything in
          my name.
      Ask and you will receive,
      and so your joy will be complete.
25    I have been telling you all this in metaphors,
      the hour is coming
      when I shall no longer speak to you in meta-
          phors;
      but tell you about the Father in plain words.
26    When that day comes
      you will ask in my name;
      and I do not say that I shall pray to the Father
          for you,
27    because the Father himself loves you
      for loving me
      and believing that I came from God.
28    I came from the Father and have come into the
          world
      and now I leave the world to go to the Father."

29    His disciples said, "Now you are speaking
30 plainly and not using metaphors! ·Now we see
      that you know everything, and do not have to
      wait for questions to be put into words; because
31 of this we believe that you came from God." ·Je-
      sus answered them:

      "Do you believe at last?
32    Listen; the time will come—in fact it has come
          already—
      when you will be scattered, each going his own
          way

and leaving me alone.
And yet I am not alone,
because the Father is with me.
33    I have told you all this
so that you may find peace in me.
In the world you will have trouble,
but be brave:
I have conquered the world."


✠


A new discourse or fragment of discourse begins
with the second half of verse 4. It covers much of the
same ground as chapter 14 does but with a different development of the themes and with some different emphases. Evidence that this is a separate treatment of the
themes may be found at the outset when Jesus comments that no one asks where he is going (verse 5).
Actually Peter has asked this in so many words
(13:36) and Thomas has in a less direct manner
(14:5). The contradiction is less glaring if we suppose
this is another version of the earlier farewell discourse.

It is somewhat startling to hear Jesus say, "It is for
your own good that I am going" (verse 7), but the sequel explains the remark. In order for the disciples to
carry out their mission, they must be aided by the
Paraclete, and Jesus has promised to send the Paraclete
only when he himself departs. The last discussion of the
Paraclete (verses 7–15) is the most extensive. It portrays the Spirit in the two major roles connected with
the designation Paraclete: a juridical role over against
the world (see 15:26–27) and an instructional role
with regard to the church (see 14:26).

Verses 8–11 are in general clear but are very difficult to understand in detail. The translation above is an interpretative one that is plausible. The Paraclete will deal with three major issues of Jesus' own preaching throughout the Gospel. Sin is understood as refusal to believe. "Being in the right"—the expression is not found elsewhere in John—is understood as Jesus fulfilling the revelation of his true identity by keeping his promise to return to the Father; the return is thus a kind of guarantee of the truth of his revelation. Judgment is understood as the decisive condemnation—expressed here in cosmic terms—of those who reject the revealing word. Though the Paraclete's role, to be exercised of course by the Johannine church and by the Gospel itself, is to convict the world of these things, we must suppose it is before a court of Christians. John does not predict a major change of heart on the part of the world.

Verses 12–15 reiterate the role of the Spirit in leading the disciples to understand Jesus and his message. Even though Jesus says he has more to say, we need not suppose the Paraclete is going to add to Jesus' revealing word. It is a matter of understanding, as is shown by such verses as 2:22; 12:16; 14:26.

Beginning with verse 16, Jesus speaks of his death and resurrection and uses the beautiful and powerful simile of the woman giving birth (verse 21) to contrast his followers' sorrow and joy. We will note, when considering the resurrection appearance of Jesus to the disciples, how many of the themes of the discourses, such as joy and peace, reappear there. Once sorrow is turned to joy—that is, once the disciples realize that Jesus has indeed returned to the Father—they may have full confidence in the Father's love (verse 27) and trust in his bounty.

One of the most difficult issues for the reader of the farewell discourses—as apparently for the disciples as they are portrayed hearing them—is to keep straight the language of Jesus' coming and going. On the one hand, his death is his return to the Father; on the other his resurrection is in some sense a return to the disciples, though in this chapter the language used is exclusively that of "seeing" Jesus. Some interpreters think there is also in the discourses mention of Jesus' second coming at the end of time, the parousia (e.g., 14:3), but even in this instance it is possible to think of the resurrection appearances. Jesus does come to the disciples after the resurrection. From then on, guided to the truth by the Paraclete and enjoying the gift of eternal life, their relationship to Jesus and the Father is as described in the farewell discourses.

The conclusion to the present discourse (verses 29–33) contains both a confession of faith on the part of the disciples and a prediction of their abandoning Jesus in the passion. Are the two compatible? Once again Jesus questions the adequacy of their faith. They believe that Jesus came from God; only after the death and resurrection, the glorification of Jesus, will they be able to believe that he has returned to the Father. True christological faith in the Fourth Gospel involves believing both movements of the pattern of Christology, descent and reascent.

STUDY QUESTIONS: According to John, what is the basis for confidence in prayer? How is joy compatible with the suffering promised in the previous section?

## John 17:1–26
## MAY THEY ALL BE ONE

17 After saying this, Jesus raised his eyes to heaven and said:

1    "Father, the hour has come:
     glorify your Son
     so that your Son may glorify you;

2    and, through the power over all mankind that
          you have given him,
     let him give eternal life to all those you have
          entrusted to him.

3    And eternal life is this:
     to know you,
     the only true God,
     and Jesus Christ whom you have sent.

4    I have glorified you on earth
     and finished the work
     that you gave me to do.

5    Now, Father, it is time for you to glorify me
     with that glory I had with you
     before ever the world was.

6    I have made your name known
     to the men you took from the world to give me.
     They were yours and you gave them to me,
     and they have kept your word.

7    Now at last they know
     that all you have given me comes indeed from
          you;

8    for I have given them
the teaching you gave to me,
and they have truly accepted this, that I came
    from you,
and have believed that it was you who sent me.

9    I pray for them;
I am not praying for the world
but for those you have given me,
because they belong to you:

10    all I have is yours
and all you have is mine,
and in them I am glorified.

11    I am not in the world any longer,
but they are in the world,
and I am coming to you.
Holy Father,
keep those you have given me true to your
    name,
so that they may be one like us.

12    While I was with them,
I kept those you had given me true to your
    name.
I have watched over them and not one is lost
except the one who chose to be lost,
and this was to fulfill the scriptures.

13    But now I am coming to you
and while still in the world I say these things
to share my joy with them to the full.

14    I passed your word on to them,
and the world hated them,
because they belong to the world
no more than I belong to the world.

15    I am not asking you to remove them from the
    world,
but to protect them from the evil one.

16    They do not belong to the world
any more than I belong to the world.

17    Consecrate them in the truth;
your word is truth.

18   As you sent me into the world,
     I have sent them into the world,
19   and for their sake I consecrate myself
     so that they too may be consecrated in truth.
20   I pray not only for these,
     but for those also
     who through their words will believe in me.
21   May they all be one.
     Father, may they be one in us,
     as you are in me and I am in you,
     so that the world may believe it was you who
         sent me.
22   I have given them the glory you gave to me,
     that they may be one as we are one.
23   With me in them and you in me,
     may they be so completely one
     that the world will realize that it was you who
         sent me
     and that I have loved them as much as you
         loved me.
24   Father,
     I want those you have given me
     to be with me where I am,
     so that they may always see the glory
     you have given me
     because you loved me
     before the foundation of the world.
25   Father, Righteous One,
     the world has not known you,
     but I have known you,
     and these have known
     that you have sent me.
26   I have made your name known to them
     and will continue to make it known,
     so that the love with which you loved me may
         be in them,
     and so that I may be in them."

✠

The farewell discourses end, as is fitting for a testament, with a majestic prayer of Jesus, which takes up again some of the themes that pervade the earlier discourses. The chapter is deservedly a favorite because of the admirable poetic simplicity of its language and because it portrays Jesus' ultimate concern not only for his disciples but for Christians of the future. Traditionally it has been called the priestly or high-priestly prayer of Jesus, because it is a prayer of intercession for others. The model is Jesus the high priest of the Epistle to the Hebrews who intercedes for the people (e.g., Heb 7:25). But even though verses 17–19 use the language of "consecration," which is sometimes used in the context of sacrifice, we should hesitate to attribute to the Fourth Gospel a Christology of priesthood.

The prayer is so carefully composed that one would expect to find a careful structure in it, but there is little agreement on what that structure is. We comment on it here by dividing simply according to the persons or groups prayed for.

Verses 1–5 are a prayer for Jesus himself, that God will crown the work Jesus has undertaken at his command, that is, glorify Jesus. The perspective is still that of the passion-resurrection both future and past. Jesus has finished the work, though he has not yet returned to the Father. Jesus also prays that he may confer the gift of eternal life, which is here defined as knowing God and Jesus.

Verses 6–19 center on the disciples, for whom Jesus prays explicitly from verse 9 on. The petitions of the prayer are that God will keep the disciples faithful to himself as Jesus has done thus far, and that God will protect them in a hostile world. The phrase "so that

they may be one like us" at the end of verse 11 is missing in some important ancient manuscripts and translations of John and probably does not belong here. The
unity of the disciples has never been in question in the
Gospel.

Verses 20–23 are an explicit prayer for the Christians of the evangelist's own time, who have come to
faith through the word, the preaching, of the disciples.
In their case Jesus prays emphatically for their unity,
which will indicate to the world that Jesus' mission was
really from God. The basis of Christian unity for John
is the unity of Father and Son and the mutual relationship of Jesus and believers, and thus that unity can
be a public sign of God's love for Jesus and Jesus' love
for his followers.

Verses 24–26 conclude the prayer with a petition for
continued union between Jesus and his followers even
after he returns to the Father. Again the relationship is
defined as one of love and indwelling.

STUDY QUESTIONS: In what respects can Jesus' prayer
serve as a model of Christian
prayer? How important to contemporary Christians is, or should be,
unity among them? What kind of
unity is desirable?

# John 18:1–27
## WHY DO YOU STRIKE ME?

1 After he had said all this Jesus left with his disciples and crossed the Kedron valley. There was a garden there, and he went into it 2 with his disciples. ·Judas the traitor knew the place well, since Jesus had often met his disciples 3 there, ·and he brought the cohort to this place together with a detachment of guards sent by the chief priests and the Pharisees, all with lanterns 4 and torches and weapons. ·Knowing everything that was going to happen to him, Jesus then came forward and said, "Who are you looking for?" 5 They answered, "Jesus the Nazarene." He said, "I am he." Now Judas the traitor was standing 6 among them. ·When Jesus said, "I am he," they 7 moved back and fell to the ground. ·He asked them a second time, "Who are you looking for?" 8 They said, "Jesus the Nazarene." ·"I have told you that I am he," replied Jesus. "If I am the one 9 you are looking for, let these others go." ·This was to fulfill the words he had spoken, "Not one of those you gave me have I lost."

10 Simon Peter, who carried a sword, drew it and wounded the high priest's servant, cutting off his 11 right ear. The servant's name was Malchus. ·Jesus said to Peter, "Put your sword back in its scabbard; am I not to drink the cup that the Father has given me?"

¹²    The cohort and its captain and the Jewish
¹³ guards seized Jesus and bound him. ·They took
him first to Annas, because Annas was the father-
in-law of Caiaphas, who was high priest that year.
¹⁴ It was Caiaphas who had suggested to the Jews,
"It is better for one man to die for the people."

¹⁵    Simon Peter, with another disciple, followed
Jesus. This disciple, who was known to the high
priest, went with Jesus into the high priest's pal-
¹⁶ ace, ·but Peter stayed outside the door. So the
other disciple, the one known to the high priest,
went out, spoke to the woman who was keeping
¹⁷ the door and brought Peter in. ·The maid on duty
at the door said to Peter, "Aren't you another of
that man's disciples?" He answered, "I am not."
¹⁸ Now it was cold, and the servants and guards had
lit a charcoal fire and were standing there warming themselves; so Peter stood there too, warming
himself with the others.

¹⁹    The high priest questioned Jesus about his dis-
²⁰ ciples and his teaching. ·Jesus answered, "I have
spoken openly for all the world to hear; I have always taught in the synagogue and in the Temple
where all the Jews meet together: I have said
²¹ nothing in secret. ·But why ask me? Ask my hear-
²² ers what I taught: they know what I said." ·At
these words, one of the guards standing by gave
Jesus a slap in the face, saying, "Is that the way
²³ to answer the high priest?" ·Jesus replied, "If there
is something wrong in what I said, point it out;
but if there is no offense in it, why do you strike
²⁴ me?" ·Then Annas sent him, still bound, to
Caiaphas the high priest.

²⁵    As Simon Peter stood there warming himself,
someone said to him, "Aren't you another of his
²⁶ disciples?" He denied it saying, "I am not." ·One
of the high priest's servants, a relation of the man
whose ear Peter had cut off, said, "Didn't I see
²⁷ you in the garden with him?" ·Again Peter denied
it; and at once a cock crew.

✠

After the very long interlude of the farewell discourses, the Gospel returns to the events of the passion narrative and moves swiftly toward its conclusion. In doing so it resumes traditional material, and the process of reinterpretation again becomes more obvious. But this is another instance where it is not easy to determine exactly what John's source is. His narrative has many points in common with Mark, but it also has a whole succession of Lukan parallels precisely where Luke differs from Mark and is widely thought to be using a separate passion story. Thus we cannot be sure whether John has an independent source for the passion or he selectively follows the same sources as the synoptic writers do. It is still helpful in highlighting John's special emphases, however, to compare with the Synoptics.

Even in the material covered in this section, from the garden scene to the interrogation before the Jewish authorities, there are some notable differences. For example, the moving story of the agony of Jesus in the garden is omitted (see comment on 12:27), no doubt in the interests of presenting Jesus as firmly in command of the decisive events. Yet a trace of the tradition remains in Jesus' remark to Peter in verse 11, "Am I not to drink the cup that the Father has given me?" Also, the Jewish interrogation of Jesus takes place not before the reigning high priest, Caiaphas, nor before the Jewish council but before the somewhat shadowy figure of Annas (verse 13). If John knew of another interrogation before Caiaphas (verse 24) he is silent about it. The minimizing of the Jewish legal or quasi-legal processes is part of the evangelist's purpose to focus on the trial before Pilate (next section). In addition to substantial differences such as these, there are numerous variations of detail in John's narrative, many of them easily explained by his overall understanding of Jesus and the passion. The reader would be helped by reading the Markan passion story (Mk 14:32 to 15:47) before proceeding further with John.

In the story of the arrest of Jesus in the garden Jesus plays a dominant role—anything but that of a helpless victim—even to the point of reducing the betrayal on Judas' part to merely pointing out where the garden was. Contrast the dramatic image of the Judas kiss in the Synoptics (see especially Lk 22:47–48). The dominance of Jesus over the whole scene comes in his use of another "I am" statement (verse 5) connoting the divine presence, before which everyone falls to the ground powerless. Not all agree that the "I am" is so significant here—it could of course mean simply "I am Jesus the Nazarene"—but one should compare 13:19, where the context alludes to the betrayal. Cross references are typical of this Gospel, whether explicit or not. Verse 9 explicitly refers to 17:12, though it interprets it somewhat less spiritually.

Peter's triple denial of Jesus is woven together with the interrogation before the Jewish authorities, as it is also in Mark, though not in precisely the same way. The "other disciple" who witnesses the interrogation is generally thought to be the "beloved disciple," who is at the origin of the Johannine traditions. The power of this complex scene speaks for itself in John as in all the Gospels.

STUDY QUESTION: Betrayal of Jesus or denial of him
                are still not uncommon reactions of
                Christians under stress. What can
                we learn from this unhappy aspect
                of the passion story?

# John 18:28 to 19:16a
## MINE IS NOT A KINGDOM
## OF THIS WORLD

28 They then led Jesus from the house of Caiaphas to the Praetorium. It was now morning. They did not go into the Praetorium themselves or they would be defiled and unable to eat the passover.
29 So Pilate came outside to them and said, "What charge do you bring against this man?" They re-
30 plied, ·"If he were not a criminal, we should not
31 be handing him over to you." ·Pilate said, "Take him yourselves, and try him by your own Law." The Jews answered, "We are not allowed to put
32 a man to death." ·This was to fulfill the words Jesus had spoken indicating the way he was going to die.

33 So Pilate went back into the Praetorium and called Jesus to him, "Are you the king of the
34 Jews?" he asked. ·Jesus replied, "Do you ask this of your own accord, or have others spoken to you
35 about me?" ·Pilate answered, "Am I a Jew? It is your own people and the chief priests who have handed you over to me: what have you done?"
36 Jesus replied, "Mine is not a kingdom of this world; if my kingdom were of this world, my men would have fought to prevent my being surrendered to the Jews. But my kingdom is not of this
37 kind." ·"So you are a king then?" said Pilate. "It

is you who say it," answered Jesus. "Yes, I am a king. I was born for this, I came into the world for this: to bear witness to the truth; and all who are on the side of truth listen to my voice." 38 "Truth?" said Pilate, "What is that?"; and with that he went out again to the Jews and said, "I 39 find no case against him. ·But according to a custom of yours I should release one prisoner at the Passover; would you like me, then, to release the 40 king of the Jews?" ·At this they shouted: "Not this man," they said, "but Barabbas." Barabbas was a brigand.

1,2 **19** Pilate then had Jesus taken away and scourged; ·and after this, the soldiers twisted some thorns into a crown and put it on 3 his head, and dressed him in a purple robe. ·They kept coming up to him and saying, "Hail, king of the Jews!"; and they slapped him in the face. 4 Pilate came outside again and said to them, "Look, I am going to bring him out to you to 5 let you see that I find no case." ·Jesus then came out wearing the crown of thorns and the purple 6 robe. Pilate said, "Here is the man." ·When they saw him the chief priests and the guards shouted, "Crucify him! Crucify him!" Pilate said, "Take him yourselves and crucify him: I can find no case 7 against him." ·"We have a Law," the Jews replied, "and according to that Law he ought to die, because he has claimed to be the Son of God."

8 When Pilate heard them say this his fears in- 9 creased. ·Re-entering the Praetorium, he said to Jesus, "Where do you come from?" But Jesus 10 made no answer. ·Pilate then said to him, "Are you refusing to speak to me? Surely you know I have power to release you and I have power to 11 crucify you?" ·"You would have no power over me," replied Jesus, "if it had not been given you from above; that is why the one who handed me over to you has the greater guilt."

12 From that moment Pilate was anxious to set

him free, but the Jews shouted, "If you set him
free you are no friend of Caesar's; anyone who
13 makes himself king is defying Caesar." ·Hearing
these words, Pilate had Jesus brought out, and
seated himself on the chair of judgment at a place
14 called the Pavement, in Hebrew Gabbatha. ·It was
Passover Preparation Day, about the sixth hour.
"Here is your king," said Pilate to the Jews.
15 "Take him away, take him away!" they said.
"Crucify him!" "Do you want me to crucify your
king?" said Pilate. The chief priests answered,
16 "We have no king except Caesar." ·So in the end
Pilate handed him over to them to be crucified.

☩

The trial of Jesus before Pilate is clearly the center-
piece of the Johannine passion narrative. It brings the
theme of judgment that has pervaded the Gospel to a
startling climax with fine dramatic power and the most
biting irony in the Gospel. It is easy to see that the
evangelist wants to highlight it. First, he has greatly expanded the brief dialogue between Jesus and Pilate into
two substantial scenes. Second, with complete disregard
for the historical situation, he has displaced the mock-
ing and scourging of Jesus, which should follow the
trial as part of the punishment, and put it in the center
of the trial. Thirdly, he has again used the technique of
the stage to structure the whole incident. The result is
very similar to the dramatic structure of chapter 9, but
the organizing principle is the frequent change of scene
from outside Pilate's official chambers, the Praetorium,
to inside and back again. The device is explained, not
implausibly, by the Jews' reluctance to incur ritual

defilement (18:28). If we note the words indicating going out and going in, we observe the following structure:

| A  | 28–32   | Outside.   | The charge: Jesus must die |
| B  | 33–38a  | Inside.    | Interrogation: kingship |
| C  | 38b–40  | Outside.   | Declaration of innocence; Barabbas |
| D  | 1–3     | (Inside.)  | Mocking of the king |
| C' | 4–8     | Outside.   | Declaration of innocence; Ecce homo |
| B' | 9–12    | Inside.    | Interrogation: power |
| A' | 13–16a  | Outside.   | The verdict: Jesus will die |

Of course, John is not a script writer and hence is not concerned with stage directions. But he uses dramatic technique very effectively in his narrative. The scenes he portrays have a certain symmetrical structure which enhances the development of plot while giving some prominence to the central scene. In fact the theme of kingship plays a dominant role in the passage, occurring in every scene but the first. Only in the central scene does anyone actually acknowledge Jesus' kingship. There, with consummate dramatic irony, the soldiers hail Jesus as king in a moment of utter human degradation.

An effective drama has more than one plot. Sometimes, as here, all the characters have their own. We can comment briefly on this passage by following the various plots in summary fashion. The careful reader will note many more details that cannot be mentioned here.

Pilate's drama is that of a representative of "the world," in the Johannine sense, who tries to avoid get-

ting involved with the revealing word of God in Jesus
and finds that neutrality is not possible. His job is to
judge, and though he seeks to evade it, not even formally pronouncing a verdict or a sentence, he cannot.
In the process he undergoes judgment himself, as everyone does in the presence of Jesus. Note how the
term "hand over" is used in the passage; it is the term
used for the betrayal on the part of Judas and had become almost a technical term in Christian circles. The
Jews "hand over" Jesus to Pilate (18:30), and Pilate
and Jesus both discuss this action (18:35 and 36, "surrendered"). In the second interrogation scene Jesus de-
clares that the "greater guilt" ("sin" in Greek) is that
of the one who hands him over (19:11). Finally,
trapped by his refusal to judge, Pilate himself "handed
him over to them to be crucified" (19:16).

"The Jews" are of course by this time in the Gospel
resolutely opposed to accepting Jesus as the Messiah-
King. They are the antagonists of the play whose
mounting, almost frenzied opposition to Jesus leads
them to an ultimate denial of the very religious values
they seek to protect. They are portrayed as concerned
with ritual purity (18:28) and the Law (19:7) but
motivated by their rejection of Jesus' revelation of God
in himself (19:7). And in the end they deny the messianic hopes they sought to defend: "We have no king
except Caesar" (19:15).

Jesus' drama lies in the irony of the situation. As the
reader knows, he really is the Messiah-King, but his is
not a kingdom of this world but a kingdom of truth
(18:36–37). He is on trial, but in reality he is the
judge, whose word provokes judgment wherever it is
heard. Pilate taunts Jesus' adversaries by displaying
him as a mock king and—perhaps with another bit of

theological irony—calling attention to his humanity: "Here is the man" (19:5). The final scene can be read somewhat differently: "Pilate had Jesus brought out, and sat *him* on the chair of judgment" (19:13). On this reading (which is grammatically quite possible), Pilate again taunts the Jews, and the sight elicits their horrifying cry. But unwittingly he places Jesus in the role of judge before whom the Jews condemn themselves by denying their messianic hope, and Pilate condemns himself by becoming a betrayer. And the inevitable result also takes place: Jesus will be crucified.

STUDY QUESTIONS:   Why can't "the world," like Pilate, remain indifferent to the revealing word of God? Are there even situations in which the stubborn defense of religious positions leads to an implicit denial of them? Why does John in this story subtly and perhaps ironically emphasize the humanity of Jesus?

## John 19:16b–42
# THEY WILL LOOK ON THE ONE WHOM THEY HAVE PIERCED

17     They then took charge of Jesus, ·and carrying his own cross he went out of the city to the place of the skull or, as it was called in Hebrew, Gol-
18 gotha, ·where they crucified him with two others,
19 one on either side with Jesus in the middle. ·Pilate wrote out a notice and had it fixed to the cross; it
20 ran: "Jesus the Nazarene, King of the Jews." ·The notice was read by many of the Jews, because the place where Jesus was crucified was not far from the city, and the writing was in Hebrew, Latin and
21 Greek. ·So the Jewish chief priests said to Pilate, "You should not write 'King of the Jews,' but
22 'This man said: I am King of the Jews.'" ·Pilate answered, "What I have written, I have written."

23     When the soldiers had finished crucifying Jesus they took his clothing and divided it into four shares, one for each soldier. His undergarment was seamless, woven in one piece from neck to
24 hem; ·so they said to one another, "Instead of tearing it, let's throw dice to decide who is to have it." In this way the words of scripture were fulfilled:

> They shared out my clothing among them.
> They cast lots for my clothes.

This is exactly what the soldiers did.

25    Near the cross of Jesus stood his mother and
his mother's sister, Mary the wife of Clopas, and
26 Mary of Magdala. ·Seeing his mother and the disciple he loved standing near her, Jesus said to his
27 mother, "Woman, this is your son." ·Then to the
disciple he said, "This is your mother." And from
that moment the disciple made a place for her in
his home.

28    After this, Jesus knew that everything had now
been completed, and to fulfill the scripture per-
fectly he said:

"I am thirsty."

29    A jar full of vinegar stood there, so putting a
sponge soaked in the vinegar on a hyssop stick
30 they held it up to his mouth. ·After Jesus had
taken the vinegar he said, "It is accomplished";
and bowing his head he gave up his spirit.

31    It was Preparation Day, and to prevent the
bodies remaining on the cross during the sabbath
—since that sabbath was a day of special solemnity
—the Jews asked Pilate to have the legs broken
32 and the bodies taken away. ·Consequently the
soldiers came and broke the legs of the first man
who had been crucified with him and then of the
33 other. ·When they came to Jesus, they found he
was already dead, and so instead of breaking his
34 legs ·one of the soldiers pierced his side with a
lance; and immediately there came out blood and
35 water. ·This is the evidence of one who saw it—
trustworthy evidence, and he knows he speaks the
truth—and he gives it so that you may believe as
36 well. ·Because all this happened to fulfill the words
of scripture:

Not one bone of his will be broken,

37 and again, in another place scripture says:

They will look on the one whom they have
    pierced.

<sup>38</sup>     After this, Joseph of Arimathaea, who was a
disciple of Jesus—though a secret one because he
was afraid of the Jews—asked Pilate to let him
remove the body of Jesus. Pilate gave permission,
<sup>39</sup> so they came and took it away. ·Nicodemus came
as well—the same one who had first come to Jesus
at nighttime—and he brought a mixture of myrrh
and aloes, weighing about a hundred pounds.
<sup>40</sup> They took the body of Jesus and wrapped it with
the spices in linen cloths, following the Jewish
<sup>41</sup> burial custom. ·At the place where he had been
crucified there was a garden, and in this garden
a new tomb in which no one had yet been buried.
<sup>42</sup> Since it was the Jewish Day of Preparation and
the tomb was near at hand, they laid Jesus there.

✠

The remainder of the Johannine passion narrative,
basically the crucifixion, death, and burial of Jesus, is a
mixture of elements of the common gospel tradition, all
reinterpreted, and incidents peculiar to the Fourth Gospel. Sometimes even the order in which things are mentioned is quite different (within the limitations of the
story, of course). It is possible that the evangelist is
adapting them to a literary structure here, but it is less
easy to detect one.

What should strike the reader most of all is the sharp
difference in the tone of the narrative when compared
with any of the Synoptics. In John there is a distinct air
of majesty, of serenity, and of course of finality about
the whole Golgotha scene. The chilling details of this
scene in the synoptic tradition, such as the mockery of
the crowds, the darkness, the rending of the Temple

veil, are as it were systematically eliminated. Jesus dies, not with a loud cry as in the Synoptics, but with a decisive comment on his fulfilling his divine mission, "It is accomplished" (verse 30). Jesus is still not the victim so much as the Son of God who lays down his life. He commands the scene. Even Simon of Cyrene, who is pressed into service to carry the cross in the Synoptics, is eliminated, and Jesus carries his own cross. The fourth evangelist offers us a wholly different side of the story of the cross.

In this part of the passion tradition in all the Gospels, we become aware of how important Psalm 22 was to Christian reflection on the story (the reader should turn to Psalm 22 to see the force of this remark). We may even say that the interpretation of the psalm (and other Old Testament passages) was so inextricably bound up with the traditions about what happened at the cross that there was mutual influence in the Gospel accounts. For example, all mention that the soldiers cast lots for Jesus' garments in accordance with Psalm 22:18—and with the custom at Roman executions—but John develops the story fully to illustrate the two lines of the psalm which he quotes (verses 23–24). Jesus' remark "I am thirsty," though it is not an exact quotation, may refer to Psalm 69:21: "When I was thirsty they gave me vinegar to drink," but it also illustrates Psalm 22:15. The Markan passion places on the lips of Jesus the opening words of Psalm 22: "My God, my God, why have you deserted me?" Here, for reasons readily recognizable, John does not make use of the psalm. For other examples of Old Testament influence, see the use of Exodus 12:46 in verse 36, giving to the death of Jesus the symbolism of the Passover lamb sacrificed on the same day, and the use of Zechariah 12:10 to interpret the piercing of Jesus' side.

Numerous details of this part of chapter 19 are peculiar to John or are highly developed from mere hints in the tradition. Let us mention but a few of them. From the tradition that there were women present at the crucifixion (see, e.g., Mk 15:40) the evangelist has developed the beautiful scene in verses 25–27. It is much more than an exemplary act of filial piety on Jesus' part: To the beloved disciple, who represents the Johannine church, Jesus entrusts his mother and a new way of Christian life is about to begin.

The account of the piercing of Jesus' side and the flow of blood and water is unique to John and has always been puzzling to his readers (as 1 Jn 5:6–8 shows). Much of the Christian tradition has seen the sacraments of Eucharist and baptism symbolized here. We should be cautious about such an identification in this Gospel, however, though it is not impossible. We cannot help recalling 7:37–39 here with its image of the water, symbolizing the Spirit, flowing from Jesus' body once he has been glorified. His glorification, his return to the Father, takes place when he has shed his blood, like the Passover lamb, in death. The solemn insistence of verse 35 on the trustworthiness of this account—which may well be a later addition to the text (see 21:24)—draws attention to its importance.

Finally we may note the burial scene. John identifies the traditional Joseph of Arimathaea as a secret believer and associates with him Nicodemus, who we already suspect is one. We know from 12:42–43 what he thinks of such people. The question here is whether he intends the burial scene to mean that Joseph and Nicodemus both come out into the open with their faith in Jesus, providing an example for others in the evangelist's own time. This seems likely, for their action was a very public one. Their preparation of the body for burial has the effect of removing the reason for the women going to the tomb on Easter morning. As we shall see presently, such a reason is not mentioned in the next chapter.

STUDY QUESTIONS: When sentimentality (not true emotion!) is set aside, how should a Christian react to the cross of Christ? Is it mere rhetoric to see in the death of Jesus a source of new life?

## John 20:1–18

# SHE HAD SEEN THE LORD

1 20 It was very early on the first day of the week and still dark, when Mary of Magdala came to the tomb. She saw that the stone 2 had been moved away from the tomb ·and came running to Simon Peter and the other disciple, the one Jesus loved. "They have taken the Lord out of the tomb," she said, "and we don't know where they have put him."

3 So Peter set out with the other disciple to go 4 to the tomb. ·They ran together, but the other disciple, running faster than Peter, reached the 5 tomb first; ·he bent down and saw the linen cloths 6 lying on the ground, but did not go in. ·Simon Peter who was following now came up, went right into the tomb, saw the linen cloths on the ground, 7 and also the cloth that had been over his head; this was not with the linen cloths but rolled up in 8 a place by itself. ·Then the other disciple who had reached the tomb first also went in; he saw and he 9 believed. ·Till this moment they had failed to understand the teaching of scripture, that he must 10 rise from the dead. ·The disciples then went home again.

11 Meanwhile Mary stayed outside near the tomb, weeping. Then, still weeping, she stooped to look

<sup>12</sup> inside, ·and saw two angels in white sitting where
the body of Jesus had been, one at the head, the
<sup>13</sup> other at the feet. ·They said, "Woman, why are
you weeping?" "They have taken my Lord away,"
she replied, "and I don't know where they have
<sup>14</sup> put him." ·As she said this she turned around and
saw Jesus standing there, though she did not rec-
<sup>15</sup> ognize him. ·Jesus said, "Woman, why are you
weeping? Who are you looking for?" Supposing
him to be the gardener, she said, "Sir, if you have
taken him away, tell me where you have put him,
<sup>16</sup> and I will go and remove him." ·Jesus said,
"Mary!" She knew him then and said to him in
<sup>17</sup> Hebrew, "Rabbuni!"—which means Master. ·Jesus
said to her, "Do not cling to me, because I have
not yet ascended to the Father. But go and find
the brothers, and tell them: I am ascending to my
Father and your Father, to my God and your
<sup>18</sup> God." ·So Mary of Magdala went and told the
disciples that she had seen the Lord and that he
had said these things to her.

✠

The first major division of the final chapter of the
Gospel actually contains two separate stories—the second one, the appearance of Jesus to Mary of Magdala,
a masterpiece of Johannine art. But they are so intri-
cately woven together that we must deal with them
under one heading. First, however, a general word
about the gospel traditions concerning the resurrection
is in order. There are two types of such traditions: stories of the empty tomb in all the Gospels, and stories of
appearances of the risen Jesus in Matthew, Luke, John,
Acts, and 1 Corinthians 15:5–8. The tradition with

which John was working, we must suppose, contained
a story of the women at the empty tomb (see Mk
16:1–8) and one or more stories of appearances to the
disciples (see Lk 24:36–49). In the passage above,
John has described an empty-tomb visit on the part of
Peter and the beloved disciple, which may be an expan-
sion of the tradition, and has transformed an empty-
tomb story involving Mary into a dramatic appearance
story. Let us concentrate on a few details of each.

The byplay between Peter, acknowledged leader of
the church at large, and the beloved disciple, authority
of the Johannine church, must be significant, though it
is hard to specify with confidence (verses 3–10). The
beloved disciple clearly has the edge, in speed and in
insight, but he defers to Peter. Perhaps the Johannine
church yields something to the larger Christian movement while at the same time claiming its own spiritual
prerogatives. For the details regarding the burial cloths,
contrast 11:44.

The real issue is that the beloved disciple "saw and
believed." It is not actually said that Peter did not believe, and we need not pursue an unexpressed contrast.
But what did the beloved disciple believe? Verse 9 says
that "they had not yet understood the teaching of scripture, that he must rise from the dead" (the JB translation is too interpretative here). So presumably the disciple did not understand that Jesus had risen. In light
of other statements in the Gospel (see, e.g., the comment on 16:30), we may suppose he believed that
Jesus had indeed returned to the Father, as he had
promised. This is what constitutes true christological
faith in the Fourth Gospel. Thus the resurrection as
such is not (yet) the object of faith.

It is typical of the Fourth Gospel to alter the story of

a group of women at the tomb so that an individual is involved. Mary experiences perplexity at the empty tomb, concluding that the body has been removed. We should note that the empty tomb of itself proves nothing about the resurrection; a gardener or anyone else could have removed the body. In the synoptic tradition the empty tomb has to be interpreted by a revelation: One or more angels must reveal that it means Jesus has risen from the dead. In John the angels, part of the tradition, are present, but they serve no revealing purpose since the empty-tomb story has become an appearance story, and Jesus can speak for himself.

The evangelist uses very effectively the ancient literary device of the recognition scene, and no comment can add to its moving power. But why does Jesus say, "Do not cling to me" (verse 17)? Among many and quite diverse suggestions one commends itself: Jesus is warning Mary not to try to hold on to the Jesus she knew, for he is returning to the Father, as he said he would. To cling to the earthly Jesus would be tantamount to a faith based merely on signs, and that is not enough.

What is the Easter message to be relayed to the disciples? In the synoptic tradition it is of course "He is risen." But nowhere in John 20 is that message mentioned. Instead, the message is that Mary had seen the Lord (verse 18; see also verse 25). The focus is not on the resurrection itself but on the visual evidence that Jesus has not vanished in death but is returning to the Father as he promised: "Tell them I am ascending to my Father" (verse 17). The really striking point, however, is in the expression, used for the first time here, "my Father and your Father, my God and your God." The Father is, now that Jesus has completed the cycle of his revealing work, the Father of his followers. In other words, they can now become children of God. The assertion of the prologue (1:12) has been fulfilled: "To all who did accept him he gave power to become children of God."

STUDY QUESTIONS: Is the resurrection of Jesus a matter of faith or of reason? How essential for the modern Christian is the empty-tomb tradition? Another way of putting this question is: What is the relationship between our view of human nature and our Christian faith in resurrection?

## John 20:19–31
# HAPPY ARE THOSE WHO HAVE NOT SEEN

¹⁹ In the evening of that same day, the first day of
the week, the doors were closed in the room where
the disciples were, for fear of the Jews. Jesus came
and stood among them. He said to them, "Peace
²⁰ be with you," ·and showed them his hands and
his side. The disciples were filled with joy when
²¹ they saw the Lord, ·and he said to them again,
"Peace be with you.

"As the Father sent me,
so am I sending you."

²² After saying this he breathed on them and said:

"Receive the Holy Spirit.
²³ For those whose sins you forgive,
they are forgiven;
for those whose sins you retain,
they are retained."

²⁴ Thomas, called the Twin, who was one of the
Twelve, was not with them when Jesus came.
²⁵ When the disciples said, "We have seen the Lord,"
he answered, "Unless I see the holes that the nails
made in his hands and can put my finger into the
holes they made, and unless I can put my hand
²⁶ into his side, I refuse to believe." ·Eight days later
the disciples were in the house again and Thomas

was with them. The doors were closed, but Jesus
came in and stood among them. "Peace be with
27 you," he said. ·Then he spoke to Thomas, "Put
your finger here; look, here are my hands. Give
me your hand; put it into my side. Doubt no
28 longer but believe." ·Thomas replied, "My Lord
29 and my God!" ·Jesus said to him:

"You believe because you can see me.
Happy are those who have not seen and yet
believe."

30 There were many other signs that Jesus worked
and the disciples saw, but they are not recorded
31 in this book. ·These are recorded so that you may
believe that Jesus is the Christ, the son of God,
and that believing this you may have life through
his name.

✠

The last two appearances of the risen Jesus in the
main body of the Fourth Gospel also serve to make
specific points besides demonstrating to the disciples
that Jesus is risen. The latter purpose as such is not actually mentioned at all. Both times the disciples are in
rooms with closed doors; yet Jesus "came" to them and
showed the identifying marks of his crucified body.
Jesus has now ascended to the Father—the ascension as
a distinct episode is Lukan, not Johannine—and can
come to the disciples to let them *see* him as he promised (see 16:16 and the comment there). It is really
Jesus, but the Fourth Gospel (unlike 1 Co 15) has
no speculation about the nature of a risen body.

The first appearance to the disciples echoes many

themes from the farewell discourses which have the cumulative effect of showing that what Jesus has promised proves to be fulfilled. We list some of these themes here with sample references to the discourses:

Jesus came: 14:18
Peace be with you: 14:27; 16:33
filled with joy: 15:11; 16:20–22
they saw the Lord: 16:16–19
I am sending you: 17:18
receive the Holy Spirit: 14:16–17, 26
sin: 15:22–24; 16:8–9

In the gospel traditions the resurrection appearance of Jesus to the disciples regularly contained the element of commissioning them to undertake the task of evangelizing (see Mt 28:18–20; Lk 24:47; Ac 1:8). In John the commission is in terms of forgiving or retaining sins (verse 23). In view of its close affinity to Matthew 16:19 and 18:18, this saying must have originally referred to the practice of early Christian churches. But does John mean simply to reaffirm that practice, which otherwise is not hinted at in his Gospel? Given the context of the saying as a postresurrection commissioning of the disciples, and given the special Johannine use of "sin" as rejection of belief in Jesus (singular and plural are interchangeable, 8:21–24), we may suppose Jesus is referring here to the general mission of his followers to share in his work of confronting people with the revealing word to provoke faith or rejection ("sin").

"Doubting Thomas" has long been a fixed part of our vocabulary. But it may be that mere doubt is not a good description of his role when we see him in the

light of Johannine thought. In his statement in verse 25
he does not just doubt, he refuses to believe. In demanding physical contact with Jesus he actually sets up
the conditions for a faith based merely on signs. He becomes one of those whom Jesus had referred to when
he said: "So you will not believe unless you see signs
and portents!" (4:48). Yet when Jesus confronts him,
it is not said that he wants any longer to fulfill his conditions, that is, he does not have to actually touch
Jesus. Instead he sees him and responds to his word
with a very lofty confession of christological faith, the
most explicit attribution of divinity to Jesus in the Gospel. Thus Thomas is more than a doubter, and we
should translate Jesus' command to him more strongly
than the JB does: "Do not be an unbeliever but a
believer!" (verse 27).

Thomas has another function, however. He is one
who must see in order to believe. Seeing Jesus is of
course not unimportant, since the disciples' experience
is the witness at the root of the Gospel. But the Gospel
is addressed to a generation of Christians who have not
seen Jesus and must rely on the word of the Gospel itself. Thus the story of Thomas provides a setting for
Jesus' final words, which are stated solemnly in the
form of a beatitude: "Happy are those who have not
seen and yet believe" (verse 29).

Verses 30–31 are a formal conclusion to the Gospel
which, because it mentions "signs," has often been
thought of as originally a conclusion to a collection of
miracle stories used in the Johannine community.
Whether that is so or not, the evangelist has used it to
conclude the Gospel, and it does so appropriately. Note
that it places the emphasis on why the Gospel was *written,* not why the events happened. But on reflection the

two are not distinct. Aided by the Spirit of truth, the evangelist has written to do what Jesus' revealing word was meant to do: to elicit faith and thus make eternal life possible.

STUDY QUESTIONS: What implications for Christian life does faith in Jesus as risen have? In what sense would John agree with Paul that "if Christ has not been raised, then our preaching is useless and your faith is useless" (1 Co 15:14)?

*Appendix*
John 21:1–25

## John 21:1–25
## FEED MY SHEEP

1 Later on, Jesus showed himself again to
21 the disciples. It was by the Sea of Tiberias,
2 and it happened like this: ·Simon Peter, Thomas
called the Twin, Nathanael from Cana in Galilee,
the sons of Zebedee and two more of his disciples
3 were together. ·Simon Peter said, "I'm going fish-
ing." They replied, "We'll come with you." They
went out and got into the boat but caught nothing
that night.

4 It was light by now and there stood Jesus on
the shore, though the disciples did not realize that
5 it was Jesus. ·Jesus called out, "Have you caught
anything, friends?" And when they answered,
6 "No," ·he said, "Throw the net out to starboard
and you'll find something." So they dropped the
net, and there were so many fish that they could
7 not haul it in. ·The disciple Jesus loved said to
Peter, "It is the Lord." At these words "It is the
Lord," Simon Peter, who had practically nothing
on, wrapped his cloak around him and jumped
8 into the water. ·The other disciples came on in
the boat, towing the net and the fish; they were
only about a hundred yards from land.

9 As soon as they came ashore they saw that
there was some bread there, and a charcoal fire
10 with fish cooking on it. ·Jesus said, "Bring some

11 of the fish you have just caught." ·Simon Peter
went aboard and dragged the net to the shore, full
of big fish, one hundred and fifty-three of them;
and in spite of there being so many the net was
12 not broken. ·Jesus said to them, "Come and have
breakfast." None of the disciples was bold enough
to ask, "Who are you?"; they knew quite well it
13 was the Lord. ·Jesus then stepped forward, took
the bread and gave it to them, and the same with
14 the fish. ·This was the third time that Jesus showed
himself to the disciples after rising from the dead.

15      After the meal Jesus said to Simon Peter,
"Simon son of John, do you love me more than
these others do?" He answered, "Yes Lord, you
know I love you." Jesus said to him, "Feed my
16 lambs." ·A second time he said to him, "Simon
son of John, do you love me?" He replied, "Yes,
Lord, you know I love you." Jesus said to him,
17 "Look after my sheep." ·Then he said to him a
third time, "Simon son of John, do you love me?"
Peter was upset that he asked him the third time,
"Do you love me?" and said, "Lord, you know
everything; you know I love you." Jesus said to
him, "Feed my sheep.

18      "I tell you most solemnly,
        when you were young
        you put on your own belt
        and walked where you liked;
        but when you grow old
        you will stretch out your hands,
        and somebody else will put a belt around you
        and take you where you would rather not go."

19 In these words he indicated the kind of death by
which Peter would give glory to God. After this
he said, "Follow me."

20      Peter turned and saw the disciple Jesus loved
following them—the one who had leaned on his
breast at the supper and had said to him, "Lord,
21 who is it that will betray you?" ·Seeing him, Peter

22 said to Jesus, "What about him, Lord?" ·Jesus
   answered, "If I want him to stay behind till I
   come, what does it matter to you? You are to fol-
23 low me." ·The rumor then went out among the
   brothers that this disciple would not die. Yet Jesus had not said to Peter, "He will not die," but,
   "If I want him to stay behind till I come."

24    This disciple is the one who vouches for these
   things and has written them down, and we know
   that his testimony is true.

25    There were many other things that Jesus did; if
   all were written down, the world itself, I suppose,
   would not hold all the books that would have to
   be written.

☩

We have already indicated briefly in the Introduction
why chapter 21 cannot be regarded as an original part
of the Fourth Gospel. It should not for that reason be
treated lightly, however. It has a narrative power not
unlike that of the Gospel itself, though it introduces a
number of puzzles for the reader. The chapter consists
basically of a third resurrection appearance of Jesus to
a group of disciples (verse 14). More precisely, it contains a miraculous catch of fish coupled with a recognition of the risen Jesus (verses 1–8), a meal with Jesus
(verses 9–14), a commissioning of Peter to be responsible for the church (verses 15–17), a prediction of
Peter's martyrdom (verses 18–19), a discussion about
the implied death of the beloved disciple (verses
20–23), and a new conclusion to the Gospel (verses
24–25). What is hardest to fathom in all this is what
really holds it together and why it was appended to the

completed Gospel. Some of these issues have implications for the life of the Johannine community and its relationship to the larger Christian church, of which Peter is seen as the leader or representative, and in that consideration may lie a reason for the chapter.

In verse 24 the Johannine community speaks in the plural "we" about the beloved disciple as author of the Gospel. Though the verse implies that he wrote what precedes immediately, it is nevertheless uncertain whether the same evangelist wrote both the Gospel and the appendix. Verses 20–23 make sense only if the beloved disciple has already died. But whoever wrote the latter was also an interpreter of earlier traditions. For the miraculous catch of fish, he knew a story similar to that in Luke 5:1–11, which has many points in common with John 21. In Luke the story is a vocation story, calling Peter to become a fisherman of people (compare the "follow me" in 21:19), but it may originally have been a resurrection appearance transformed into something else by Luke. Possibly the author of chapter 21 also knew the tradition of a resurrection appearance to Peter (see Lk 24:34; 1 Co 15:15).

Traditional interpretation has seen a number of symbolisms in details of this chapter. In verse 7, for example, the fact that the beloved disciple is first to recognize the risen Jesus suggests the superior spiritual insight of the Johannine church (see 20:8). The precise number of fish, 153, is so unusual as to be significant (verse 11), and guessing its meaning has always been tantalizing. For many it suggests the inclusiveness of the church. The meal of bread and fish (verse 13) reminds us of the multiplication of the loaves and is often taken as a eucharistic meal. The three-part dialogue of Jesus with Peter (verses 15–17) corresponds to Peter's triple denial, though we must note that it is the reader who makes this point, not the writer.

The second conclusion is at least to some extent imitative of the first. By its use of hyperbole, it is much less impressive than its model.

# SUGGESTED FURTHER READINGS

Contemporary literature on the Fourth Gospel is immense, at all levels of scholarly and popular style. The following brief list runs the gamut of them, beginning with two commentaries.

Brown, Raymond E. *The Gospel According to John.* The Anchor Bible. 2 volumes. Garden City, N.Y.: Doubleday, 1966, 1970. An excellent new translation with an exhaustive commentary that is scholarly and very readable. To be consulted rather than read straight through.

Lindars, Barnabas. *The Gospel of John.* New Century Bible. Greenwood, S.C.: Attic Press, 1972. A thorough commentary based on the Revised Standard Version, written with great clarity.

Barrett, C. K. *The Gospel of John and Judaism.* Philadelphia: Fortress Press, 1975. A series of scholarly lectures on a particularly difficult issue in Johannine studies.

Kysar, Robert. *John, the Maverick Gospel.* Atlanta: John Knox Press, 1976. Paper. A very attractive introduction to major issues in the theology of John, designed for students.

Kysar, Robert. *The Fourth Evangelist and His Gospel*. Minneapolis: Augsburg Publishing House, 1975. Paper. A clear and very well organized critical survey of modern scholarship on the Gospel.

MacRae, George W. *Faith in the Word: The Fourth Gospel*. Herald Biblical Booklets. Chicago: Franciscan Herald, 1973. Paper. A brief introduction to John.

Martyn, J. Louis. *History and Theology in the Fourth Gospel*. New York: Harper & Row, 1968. A very creative exploration of the significance of the Gospel for understanding Jews and Christians in the evangelist's own time.

Perkins, Pheme. *Gospel of St. John*. Read and Pray. Chicago: Franciscan Herald, 1975. Paper. Comments, reflections, and prayers based on the Gospel.

Smith, D. Moody. *John*. Proclamation Commentaries. Philadelphia: Fortress Press, 1976. Paper. A brief and insightful introduction to the Gospel and to methods of interpreting it.

Taylor, Michael J., ed. *A Companion to John*. New York: Alba House, 1977. Paper. A collection of readings in Johannine theology from a wide variety of modern scholars.

Vanderlip, D. George. *Christianity According to John*. Philadelphia: Westminster Press, 1975. A fresh examination of major themes and symbols in the Gospel.

# OTHER IMAGE BOOKS

# OTHER IMAGE BOOKS

# OTHER IMAGE BOOKS

# OTHER IMAGE BOOKS